SECURITY IN EUROPE

International Relations Series Volume 2

SECURITY IN EUROPE

Robert Hunter

ELEK BOOKS LONDON

© 1969 Robert Hunter
All rights reserved
Published in Great Britain by
Elek Books Limited
2 *All Saints Street, London, N.*1
SBN 236 17753 2

To
J. C. R.

MADE AND PRINTED IN GREAT BRITAIN BY
MORRISON AND GIBB LIMITED, LONDON AND EDINBURGH

Contents

Preface

This book on European security is intended first of all for students who began life in a world that already spelt Cold War with capital letters, and who, like me, will only know of its beginnings from their elders. If they accept what I say here as uncritically as we who grew up in the Cold War accepted what we were taught about it, then I shall be disappointed. But if it advances, even by a single step, the understanding of what is at worst called international relations and at best history, then I shall be pleased.

The ideas in this book have taken shape over many years. As a result, it would be impossible for me to thank adequately everyone who has helped me in preparing it. But in general I want to thank the Department of International Relations at the London School of Economics for seven years' careful nurturing, as well as my students, both at the LSE and in the far corners of Britain, who have borne heresy with good grace. Most of all I want to thank Philip Windsor for inspiration, guidance, and for being as good an editor as one could wish for without his actually writing the whole book himself. And my thanks to Miss Angela Hallett for typing the manuscript.

Any errors of fact are entirely my own responsibility; so is my irreverence.

> Leucis, who intended a Grand Passion,
> Ends with a willingness-to-oblige.
> (*Epitaph*, Ezra Pound)

Introduction

One of the central problems within the study of international relations concerns the whole question of security, whether of a nation, an alliance, or of the international political system as a whole. Indeed, a significant body of theory regards the gaining and preserving of security against political, economic, or military threats to be *the* central problem, in comparison with which all other aspects of international relations are relatively insignificant.

In any event, problems of security are important from any perspective. And in recent years, no context of security has seemed more important, or been more carefully analysed and organized, than that relating to Europe, both East and West. The European context has provided the central focus for Soviet-American rivalry, concern, and confrontation of one form or another; it is the arena in which both super-powers have, over the years, maintained the largest permanent commitment of forces outside their borders; and it continues to be seen by both as a vital interest.

This book is a discussion of the major problems relating to the security of Europe since the Second World War, viewed as a context that necessarily embraces the nations of the Soviet *bloc* as well as the West European Allies of the United States.

In addition, this book will attempt to place some of these problems in a wider perspective, drawing more general conclusions about the nature of security as it applies elsewhere in the world. To do this will require a discussion of several important factors that have defined the nature of the Cold War in Europe, shaped its course, and prescribed the requirements for its end.

To begin with, nothing existed in the early days following

the end of the Second World War that made a Cold War in Europe inevitable. It is true that there had been a considerable period of history during which Europe had posed serious security problems of one sort or another, and evoked formal responses, whether a loosely-structured balance of power system, a network of alliances, or the highly-structured League of Nations. But for there to be a repetition of these patterns in Europe in the late 1940s—or, indeed, for them to be introduced elsewhere in the world—depended upon certain assumptions. First, statesmen had to believe that there was some *absence* of security—and this is as much a psychological as a physical state in any situation where there is no actual aggression. In post-war Europe, this absence of security could be defined crudely as the lack of any clearly-defined rules for the conduct of political relations among states, viewed within a context in which two effectively new and inexperienced great powers, the United States and the Soviet Union, found themselves suddenly dominating the Continent of Europe. There began, therefore, a search for ways to provide these rules, or at least to reduce the uncertainty that the absence of rules presented. This was not necessarily a process conducted in a *military* dimension. Indeed, as the following discussion will point out, the problems of European security, whether viewed from the East or from the West, were at first related, not to military matters, but rather to matters of political organization and stability, as well as to pressing matters of economic recovery and strength. The military dimension of security was added only later—an addition that was, itself, a significant step in transforming a political conflict into something far more complex and demanding from the standpoint of ordering political relations on the Continent—i.e. of introducing elements of certainty and confidence into those relations.

The need for a system of security in Europe, therefore, was first of all the product of perceptions that the absence of such a system would be undesirable. This is not to argue, however, that there were no fundamental conflicts of interest, particularly as between the United States and the Soviet Union. It is only to argue that the forms that these conflicts would take, and the methods chosen to resolve them, did not necessarily require the formation of two opposing military *blocs*.

The choice of these forms and methods stemmed primarily from perceptions of threats posed to different European countries and to the political interests of the Soviet Union and the United States in Europe. It was these perceptions, or rather *misperceptions*, that shaped the structure of the Western Alliance system—NATO—and the interlocking web of treaties concluded by the Soviet Union with its satellite nations—a web of treaties later converted into the Warsaw Pact. This was not an automatic process, but rather an accumulation of discrete steps that, taken together, led political conflict from the realm of politics and economics to one whose principal dimension was military. And once that military dimension was added, it imposed a logic on events in Europe that largely eclipsed political and economic development across what had emerged as two halves of Europe, regardless of what the prospects for such development had been beforehand.

Indeed, from the time of NATO's foundation in 1949 until at least the early 1960s, the entire fabric of European security was dominated by a central paradox: that the achieving of some fixed and certain ideas about the nature of security on the Continent—ideas symbolized by the establishment of two opposing and clearly-defined *blocs*—provided both an added impetus to the Cold War and the first step towards signalling the Cold War's end. The creation of something that could be called a *status quo*, set in a formal context of East-West confrontation, provided the basis for ending those mutual hostilities that were founded on a lack of certainty about the manner in which political relations on the Continent were to be ordered. But in achieving this *status quo* through a specifically military alliance, the nations concerned with Europe's security imposed a logic of confrontation that had to be followed through, step by step, until there was a strategic stability in Europe to match

3

the political stability conferred by the very act of establishing the two *blocs*.

April 4, 1949, the day that the North Atlantic Treaty was concluded, was therefore both the final moment in the creation of a Cold War that would be conducted largely—at least by the West—in military terms, and the first moment in the process of bringing that Cold War to a close. Yet more than a decade was required to work through the appropriate logic—to achieve a strategic stability that would be equal to any perceptions of threat—after which the political stability of 1949 could be used as the basis for a political *détente* between East and West in Europe.

This process was complicated by yet another factor: the role played by the development of institutions in shaping and defining the nature of conflict in Europe and the manner in which the logic of confrontation would be carried through to its end. Indeed, it may be argued that all security problems in Europe—if not security problems in the world generally— were a compound of genuine conflicts of interest, perceptions, and institutional development. Within the Western Alliance, in particular, the internal politics of the North Atlantic Treaty Organization—especially the role played by the United States and the collateral uses for which the Alliance was designed— largely determined the way in which NATO countries interpreted the Soviet 'threat' and chose means for reacting to it. In this way the logic of confrontation acquired an extraordinary political complexity.

In the East, the web of bilateral treaties, later supplemented by the Warsaw Pact, has never become as important in the Soviet scheme of things for its Alliance system as NATO has been throughout for the United States in the West. There has been no uniform pattern over the years in the Soviet use of its Alliance, but even when most significant—as during the 1968 invasion of Czechoslovakia—the Warsaw Pact has never rivalled NATO as a means for channelling super-power influence to dependent states.

This analysis has led me to approach the problem of European security in the following manner: first, to present a sketch history of the development of confrontation in Europe after the Second World War—the essential paradox of the Cold War and its military logic.

Second, this book will discuss the nature of the concept of threat, and its relationship to the matter of perception, or misperception. Third, it will present the ways in which the development of NATO, as an institution, affected the development of the context of confrontation, and shaped Western responses within the logic imposed by that confrontation. Less will be said about similar developments in the Warsaw Pact, primarily because of the lesser role played by the Pact, as an institution, in shaping the more general context of security embracing the entire Continent.

Fourth, this book will present the basic strategic factors relating to European security problems as these strategic factors developed over the years, in terms both of the demands imposed by confrontation and of the ways in which the NATO Alliance, in particular, worked through its internal political relations through debates on what were ostensibly strategic issues. Here, again, the more important political role played by NATO as a diplomatic instrument of that Alliance's super-power, in contrast to the role played by the Warsaw Pact in Russian diplomacy, requires that greater attention be paid to NATO than to the Warsaw Pact, despite the gradual increase in the importance of the latter since the mid-1960s.

The same reasoning also applies to a short fifth section: a brief comparison of the diplomatic uses of Alliance systems, in order to highlight some of the factors common to European security and security elsewhere in the world, and also to illustrate differences. For this purpose, this study will refer to the Central Treaty Organization, another Alliance system sponsored by the United States and lending itself to comparison with NATO as an Alliance used by a super-power for diplomatic purposes, and also having its own internal 'dynamic'.

Sixth, there will be a further discussion of the diplomatic uses of alliances: in this instance, the non-military aspects of NATO. This is a topic rarely treated in detail, but which is of central importance in understanding the political context within which contemporary political, economic and strategic developments in Europe must be viewed. In particular, some of the political problems of European organization and development that were more or less submerged by the overriding context of military confrontation can be seen clearly in various efforts made over the years to use NATO for non-military purposes.

This leads naturally to the final section: a discussion about the process of *détente* in Europe, and about the resurrection of underlying political problems after the logic of military confrontation had been worked through and the Cold War came to an end. This is the culmination of nearly two decades of developing patterns in European security, and the amalgam of political, economic and strategic factors that will be relevant to changes in the present forms of confrontation across the Continent. It is the conclusion of this study that change in Europe will be largely an expression of twenty years' development in NATO and in its rival Alliance across a divided Continent.

Robert Hunter

April 1969

Chapter 1

Beginning of the Cold War

Twenty years after the North Atlantic Treaty was signed, it has become popular to look back on one of the great marvels of diplomacy—the structure called NATO, which has survived a period almost equal to that between the first and second world wars; it has given Europe a period of relative peace and security that would have seemed unreal in the context of the pre-war world; and it has continued, 24 years after the end of World War II, to keep the United States bound to the defence of a collection of European nations.

This has certainly been a success for Western diplomacy. But behind the self-congratulation also lies a large measure of misunderstanding—not least on the part of people in the fifteen countries that make up the North Atlantic Alliance. For in twenty years, the estrangements and cultural divisions that have set country apart from country, and continent apart from continent, are still apparent. This is now true in less measure perhaps, as we have seen the development of a Common Market that still retains a bit of spiritual life; yet America and France, for example, seemed farther apart in 1968 than in 1948, and Britain farther apart from either.

There are many reasons for this development, not least of which is the perception by various allies of 'closeness' or 'change' in their relations. After all, the euphoria of early co-operative ventures within NATO has given way to the familiarity that breeds contempt—there is no longer anything left of the sense of urgency which the Americans were able to convey to their potential allies in 1949. But of all the pressures that have led observers in the late 1960s to concentrate on the divisions within

NATO, one of the most important was the conventional wisdom that there should have been *unity*.

This is not an uncommon problem with any institution. But with NATO, the problem has been particularly acute, since there has always been a need—at least in times of threat—to give an *appearance* of unity that would help deter attack or at least Russian political adventures. But the sophistication of this idea has often been lost, both because the outward facade of NATO as an institution has been accepted as real, and because the high expectations held for NATO, by many well-intentioned and perhaps far-sighted people, has tended to reinforce this idea of NATO as something very special in international relations.

The NATO facade of unity and integrity has proved a particularly dangerous illusion. The Alliance has acquired buildings, a flag, uniformed military officers of fourteen nations (Iceland has no armed forces), elaborate communications, and its own glossy magazines. Indeed, over the years, a code of NATO behaviour has grown up, against which the performance of individual member states has been measured. Never mind that few countries—did any?—have ever managed to live up to major elements of the code. For instance, the number of troops maintained in readiness has usually fallen short of goals. There was still the public appearance of solidarity and normal functioning, as though NATO were practically another government with a constitution, instead of a collection of more or less sovereign states that had subscribed to a treaty, which is after all a good deal less demanding than a domestic constitution.

But through laziness, perhaps, the NATO code of desirable behaviour came to stand for reality, to such a point that the French Government's revaluation of the worth of NATO against its costs—a computation central to the continuation of any treaty arrangement—was greeted by some governments almost as though it were treason. Nor was this just a tactic designed to swing the Government of President de Gaulle back into line through an appeal to the sainted traditions of the

Alliance. There was actually a belief that the French were rupturing a code of behaviour that had value for its own sake, regardless of the purposes—military and political—that it was actually designed to serve. The French were drawing graffiti on the facade of NATO: and this was effrontery—*lèse-majesté*— quite beside any real damage that might have been done to the structure beneath.

This response was perhaps inevitable in a structure about which so much had been written and spoken in so many countries, and in whose name so much had been done, not least by heads of government who needed to appeal to some outside, almost mystical, authority to get needed appropriations out of niggardly parliaments. But there were other reasons, as well, one of which could be called a sense of tidy-mindedness, most noticeable in the Americans, that reflected again the problems of a coalition among nations basically foreign to one another. This problem recurred throughout the period of this study, and was particularly important in the Allies' discussions of the questions of the so-called Multilateral Force and nuclear sharing during the early 1960s.

The other major factor in making apostasy a crime—namely, the high expectations held for NATO—was even more important. But this subject is so intricate, and full of implications for the overall development and character of NATO and other forms of Western co-operation, that it must be reserved for a longer discussion on its own. The significant point, at this stage, is that the conventional wisdoms about NATO were themselves of considerable importance in directing its course, and, in particular, in leading to the appearance of uniformity and broad common purpose that its facade and bland communiqués seemed to indicate.

But in understanding NATO, one must go behind this facade, to probe the subtle political currents that have formed and shaped it, to examine the compromises and the ambiguities that are both the source of its unprecedented success, and the most tangible source of its later division and discord. One must begin with the nature of European security problems in the period following the Second World War, when there was no recognizable balance of power or other mechanism to give an air of certainty to political and security relationships among European states.

It has become natural for a generation growing up in the post-war world to accept the division of Europe into two *blocs* as the established order of things; to see the Iron Curtain as stretching limitlessly backwards in time (as it can be directly apprehended in one's own life); and even to accept a view that countries beyond the frontiers of the NATO countries are in permanent darkness. The division of Europe may seem the only real and hard fact in the context of European politics as conducted by the super-powers: it has been ordained that Europe should be divided—it was a natural occurrence—and all the rest can be seen in terms of preserving this division, without dangerous alterations on either side.

This is a compelling view, reinforced by the formal nature of the opposing *blocs*, and by the tangible character of the two institutions, NATO and the Warsaw Pact. But it is a view that has rarely had validity, and has always been accepted more firmly in some countries—in particular the United States— than in others. This view also belies the substance of European security, and the means by which it was achieved.

The immediate post-war period began on a note of naïve hope in the West, particularly in the United States. Perhaps with even more widespread conviction than in 1918, Americans saw the conflict just ended as the war to end wars. The principal victors, the United States and the Soviet Union, seemed to many to share a common commitment to prevent a recurrence of divisions in Europe on the questions of peace and security. The United Nations was seen as the embodiment of a new and enduring system of collective security, the forum within which the major powers would be able to make the decisions necessary to preserve world peace.

Within two years of the end of World War II, however, there

was the most profound disillusionment in the West. The Soviet Union quite obviously had different views concerning the interests that were to be confirmed by collective security arrangements. And nowhere were these differing views more apparent than in Europe, where the Western powers found what they regarded as Soviet obstruction at almost every step in trying to liquidate the legacy of confusion and political uncertainty left by the war.

The basic facts of this period are well known. But the difficulty in turning these facts into history has always lain in assigning 'blame' for the breakdown of co-operation that had been built up—and exaggerated—during the war. Until recently, Western accounts, written mainly by Americans, have tended to speak in terms of Soviet villainy, and assigned to the Russians the motives essential to the gradual establishment of a Cold War and, with it, the necessary development of a North Atlantic Alliance. But in recent years, the pendulum of analysis has swung the other way, and has led to a spate of criticisms directed at the United States—criticisms that assign to a form of American imperialism the prime motive force in breaking down Soviet-American friendship. This kind of analysis is primarily American too.

The truth of the matter is probably of less importance than the attitudes these two styles of criticism represent. In the former case, there was both a Western ideological purity and American naïvety about the limits of trust and the nature of political interests. In the latter case there has developed a sense of Western guilt in face of new evidence that detracts from earlier, uncritical rationalizations of Western action.

But aside from these problems of changing perceptions at the time—that is, the late 1940s—conflicts of interest between the Soviet Union and the United States in Europe were widely seen in terms of their detraction from an acknowledged ideal of unity. This way of looking at problems not only made the individual issues less amenable to bargaining and resolution, but it also contributed greatly to the climate in which a venture like NATO would gain support.

Soon after the end of the war, there developed disagreements over the meaning of the Yalta decisions of 1945—disagreements caused by mutual misunderstanding, distrust, Soviet expansionism, or perhaps a combination of these. Here there lay cause for concern in the West, but this did not yet mean that there should be new security arrangements, as such, for the Continent. There were widespread fears in the western part of Europe, but these were fears of communism, spurred on by economic devastation, not fears of Soviet aggression. Throughout the period in which communism was a major threat, particularly in France and Italy, little thought was given to the problems of a military nature. Among other things, it still seemed possible in Western Europe to regard Russian (or Communist) activities as ambiguous, and there was still some willingness in the West to take account of the incredible devastation visited upon the Soviet Union during the war. Indeed, one of the most significant facts about the formation of NATO is that the process began after the major internal threats to Western European countries were beginning to subside.

The political structure of the Continent, however, was missing something very real that could have prevented the onset of a Cold War and the development of opposing security organizations dividing East from West. There was, quite simply, no common understanding about the nature of security, and no certainty about the source of security in the future. One must remember, after all, that in the interwar period, there had been the most elaborate arrangements designed to preserve security—arrangements noted for their intricacy and allowing for shifts in loyalties among nations in order to preserve something of a balance of power system. And these shifts in loyalties (as with the Nazi-Soviet Pact) took place even despite the developing ideological politics of the twentieth century.

In view of the history of European Alliance systems, therefore, could one conceive, in the late 1940s, of arrangements for security in the broadest sense—some sort of certainty against the emergence of new Hitlers or the vicissitudes of power politics—that did not include firm understandings among the various European powers? In the circumstances, it is surprising that European nations continued as long as they did after the war without any such arrangements, although from the first there were formal agreements among the major powers. An Anglo-Russian treaty had been signed in 1942 and a Franco-Russian treaty in 1944. But it was not until 1947 that there was a major treaty in the West, linking France and Britain, and even here—in all three treaties—the putative aggressor was envisaged quite specifically, not as the Soviet Union or any Western power, but as a resurgent Germany.

Germany was, indeed, the key to all the security problems in Europe after the war and, in many ways, it remains the key to those problems today. Much has been written about the failure of the Western Allies to secure access rights to Berlin as part of the agreements reached at the Yalta Conference. But these discussions merely tended to obscure the very real conflicts of interest that developed over Germany among the occupying powers.

To begin with, there was the question of the psychological attitudes towards the former German aggressors held by each of the Allies. Here, American readiness to forgive actually created a source of tension. Whereas the Americans wished to avoid the problems that followed the First World War—including German revanchism that was bred by Allied insistence on reparations—the Russians retained a great reservoir of understandable bitterness. They were not alone. The French continued to regard the Germans with great suspicion, and were certainly much closer to the Russians in their attitudes on the administration of the four zones of Germany than to the Americans. This is a fact that has often been ignored in the context of Cold War oratory, and which still motivates much of French European policy, including the vaunted Franco-German treaty of rapprochement that was concluded in 1963.

American officials in those days took little account of these Russian and French sensibilities, and put them down instead to Russian expansionist aims. This is not to say that such aims were not there, but rather that the necessary dialogue—a process of bargaining over the future of Germany—was made more difficult by a philosophical difference over the treatment of the defeated enemy.

A similar problem obtained with regard to the nature of governments in European nations, and Germany in particular. Differences of attitude became apparent first with the constitution of a Government for Poland, when the Anglo-American desire for a democratic government encountered the Russian desire for regimes in eastern Europe which would be subservient to Soviet interests. Here were potent causes of mistrust. Even worse, they indicated that there was no common understanding between Russians and Americans about the nature of the security problem in Europe. For the Americans, there was only the question of trying to prevent another European war, presumably begun by Germany, that would again drag in the Americans to decide the outcome and, with it, the balance of power in the world. But for the Russians the nature of the regimes in eastern Europe—and in Germany—was of crucial importance in providing the Soviet Union with defence against attacks from the West, a much more compelling motive for security than a generalized opposition to war. It was clearly in the Russian interest to be able to create a *cordon sanitaire* in reverse, giving the Soviet Union a sure defence that the diplomacy of the 1920s and 1930s had not provided. And it is quite understandable that the Russians would see the American penchant for democracy and representative government—particularly in highly nationalistic countries like Poland that had little reason to love the Russians in 1945—as posing a threat to Russian security. Unfortunately, in the controversy, what may have been misunderstandings came to be seen by each side as deliberate attempts by the other to deny something of importance: for the Russians, their security; for the Americans, the promises made during the period of the 'Grand Alliance', to make arrangements for a firm post-war peace benefiting all the nations that had been victimized by Germany.

This problem was repeated within Germany itself. What was to become of this defeated country? In a very real sense the origins of NATO owe more to the demand for Germany's unconditional surrender—i.e. in its elimination as an 'actor' in the European arena—than to anything else. Just as the defeat of Japan led to the search in Asia for a replacement to Japanese power, so the end of German power left the entire centre of Europe in grave uncertainty about its future. Would there be another German threat? How was it to be prevented? How was this divided country to be administered? And could the German nation be administered in a way that would benefit the interests of all the major powers?

This last question was the most fateful. For as long as there was common agreement about the demands of European security—i.e. the defeat of Germany—then the actual disposition of the defeated territories was of secondary importance. But when there appeared to be no common understanding on the future of all of Europe—as the disagreement on Poland seemed to promise—then the strategic potential of Germany began almost immediately to take on importance, and has retained that importance to this day. In short, could anything be done with Germany, either as one nation, two, or four?

Still, this question might not have taken on such importance if there had not been the problem of uncertainty about future European political and economic arrangements, felt particularly acutely by the officials administering the American zone of Germany, but by no means limited to them. They exhibited a great deal of impatience to resolve the dilemmas of Germany, impatience stemming largely from very practical, humanitarian grounds: to formalize an administration, particularly a common administration, would greatly aid the problem of economic recovery. It was a worthy aim, but it conflicted directly with the Russian, and to an extent the French, insistence on security first as far as Germany was concerned. Therefore, each American attempt to institute a 'rational' process of administering the defeated enemy was greeted by the Russians with hostility and resistance, and that response in turn led the Americans to suspect Russian motives still further.

The result for Europe—and for Germany—was a gradual crystallizing of opinion in East and West of particular views about the future of the Continent and, in particular, about the future of the four (later two) zones of Germany. It may be argued that the Americans were unwilling or unable to take sufficient account of the hard strategic realities that were seen by the Russians. It may be argued, in turn, that the Russians were overly suspicious of American idealism (which would seem, to the Russians, to work in the political favour of America, as well—a view with considerable merit). But in any event the upshot was a greater desire in the West to create a degree of certainty about the future—the establishment of some framework for treating the future of Germany and Europe—and in Russia a greater desire to do likewise, except within Germany itself. Here, the Russians were content to have the future of Germany remain uncertain, just so long as it was not unified and powerful and they retained control of at least their portion. And this view came into conflict directly with the American view of the efficient administration and recovery of Germany, a view held almost without regard to the problems that this could pose in the future for all those European countries (Russia included) which had been invaded by a powerful German state.

The background to the formation of NATO can be seen as a process of misunderstanding and genuine differences of view about the manner in which the economic and political life of various European countries should be organized. But these differences of view were not so much in conflict that there need have been a division of the Continent into two hostile and armed *blocs* in order to resolve the matter. The difficulty lay, rather, in the failure of either side to clarify the terms in which they could both talk about European recovery and the future of Germany.

There were, in effect, no guidelines, except those rather haphazardly drawn up as the frontiers of military occupation during the wartime conferences. There was no firm understanding between the United States and Soviet Union about what had to be done to avoid a conflict of interest—and this was a philosophical as much as a political problem; nor were there any firm agreements on a division of political and strategic interests in Europe around which real bargaining could take place. The greatest anomaly was Germany, and with regard to Germany there lasted the longest process of trying to define the nature of European security.

Therefore, this discussion so far has illustrated what is perhaps one of the most important points to be made about the whole post-war history of European security: namely that the onset of the Cold War really reflected the inability of both Russia and America to find ways either of overcoming their misunderstandings, or of deciding where there was scope for bargaining. Having never struck a balance of advantage, they were unable to come to terms with the demands of avoiding conflict, the demands of feeling secure in a continent that had no military divisions but still had considerable uncertainty about its political future. To do otherwise was probably too much to ask of diplomats, particularly those of America and Russia who were unused to the complexities of great power responsibility. In the end, the way out of uncertainty—the gaining of a form of psychological security by bringing into being institutions of a military and political security—was the formation of opposing military alliances and the freezing of the only basis for an agreed *status quo* that seemed to exist.

Such is the stuff of Cold War—when hostility and mistrust act upon uncertainty about the balance of power. A 'context of conflict' is produced—perhaps without anyone willing it—in which the political possessions of each side are carefully husbanded, and every move of the new 'enemy' is invested, rightly or wrongly, with hostile intent. A Cold War can be avoided where the real areas of contention are clear, and the consequences of change predictable—that is, where it is clear what can be the subject of bargaining, and what cannot. But in the hostile atmosphere of a Cold War, there is no such separation of vital from negotiable interests, as the implacable nature of conflict supersedes reason in the ordering of security affairs for mutual benefit. So it is with the Americans and the Chinese, today; so it was with the Americans and the Russians in the late 1940s.

But if a Cold War begins at least in part because of uncertainty in ordering political and security affairs, the end of a Cold War requires at least the removal of that uncertainty. And this, indeed, is just what both NATO and the Soviet Alliances in Eastern Europe (later the Warsaw Pact) managed to achieve. The end of Cold War, therefore, began with the establishment of NATO, an act which gave the first concrete form to post-war security in Europe, and provided a context for approaching these problems. But, unfortunately, it took many years for this to become apparent. In particular, the anomalous status of Germany had yet to be settled, and the very establishment of a military means of reducing uncertainty in Europe (NATO) helped to increase the tensions that made any appreciation of the new 'certainty' difficult if not impossible to define.

Since that time, we have witnessed at least two phases of relaxed tensions; the 'spirit of Geneva' in 1955, and the generalized *détente* following the Cuban missile crisis in 1962. Neither period really saw a change in strategic factors; both, instead, were concerned with the way in which what were really established patterns of European division would be viewed, and the extent to which other factors—tension and threat—would impinge upon the basic elements of the strategic equation.

So next, one must consider the problem of threats, and the implications of various threats for the formation and history of NATO and European security, in general.

Chapter 2

The Threat

It is now the conventional wisdom that NATO was formed in response to a real and immediate Soviet military threat to Western Europe, and that this threat has only begun to fall off in recent years in response to the success of NATO. It would be difficult to analyse the second half of this appreciation—there is certainly some truth in it, even though perhaps not the whole truth. But the first part—the initial Soviet military threat—bears closer examination. As already suggested in Chapter 1, there was scope for misunderstanding between East and West from the end of the Second World War, and a desire for certainty in dealing with the amorphous and unstructured politics of a ravaged Continent.

But the North Atlantic Treaty was not signed until 1949, although there was a rudimentary Brussels Treaty signed by Britain, France, Belgium, the Netherlands and Luxembourg in March 1948. Indeed, there are good grounds for arguing that NATO remained little more than a diplomatic guarantee until the formation of Allied Command Europe under General Eisenhower in April 1951. How, then, did the process of the emerging Cold War (the reduction of political and strategic uncertainty in a period of misunderstanding and conflicts of interest) take on its military character?

This development was the result of a process of action and response with many factors working in one direction—i.e. towards the onset of a militarized confrontation. In Western Europe, there was indeed in the late 1940s seen to be a form of threat from the Soviet Union. That threat was not, however, seen to be of a military nature, but was rather centred on the role of internal Communist parties that were aided—as in the case of Greece, at the far edge of Europe—by outside aid and political support. And the rather belated response to these threats was contained in the Truman Doctrine and the Marshall Plan, both decidedly non-military enterprises. But almost nowhere was there a sense that the Russians would use their military superiority to attack westward. Indeed, Mr Churchill's 'Iron Curtain' speech at Fulton, Missouri, in March 1946 was greeted with cries of outrage at home—and there is reason to believe that this address was more of a self-fulfilling prophecy than a warning of potential disaster. And even then, as his phrase about the Iron Curtain indicated, Churchill was prophesying, not a Soviet advance westwards, but the division of Europe, indeed, a division running *east* of Germany. Still, it may seem natural to suppose that the creation of NATO presupposed a threat to the vital interests of Western European countries. But this assumption hides the real subtleties of European politics, in the post-war period and later.

To begin with, there was always the problem of perspective. With many countries interested in European security, each evaluating the behaviour of the Soviet Union, there would almost certainly be a divergence of opinion about what this behaviour meant, unless it turned into the most flagrant aggression. There were, indeed, such divisions of opinion, and in themselves they accounted for much of the impetus for the formation of a rigorous military alliance of twelve sovereign nations.

Throughout the history of NATO, and even before, the United States has held a more suspicious view of Soviet behaviour than has any European nation, with the exception of West Germany, which itself did not enter the Alliance until 1955. In many ways this American attitude does not represent the paradox it seems. For example, the Americans very early took primary responsibility among Western nations for dealing with the Russians on such sensitive and difficult matters as the occupation regime for Germany and the status of Berlin, about which disagreements began even before the Potsdam conference was held in the summer of 1945. Soviet intransigence—as the Americans saw it—therefore had a more profound impact in the United States than it would in European countries whose statesmen were more sceptical anyway about the possibilities of co-operation among essentially foreign nations. In that vein, the Americans held a more idealistic view of the possibilities of co-operation, and were therefore more likely to suffer profound disillusionment on this score. For this purpose—analysing Russian intentions—one may even consider Winston Churchill to be an honorary American—the self-fulfilling prophet un-honoured in his own country—and he was to be officially accorded this honorary citizenship many years later.

During the first three years after the Second World War—a period of disillusionment—a 'case' for believing in Russian aggressive and expansionist aims was gradually built up but, again, primarily in the United States, the Western country most removed from the actual scene of action, and least tutored in lessons of diplomacy. To be fair to Churchill, one must note that he did see the difficulties of dealing directly with the Soviet Union (on any basis that played down relations of power), and it was in the context of urging a particular *method* of diplomacy on the Americans that he made his single contribution to post-war thinking in his Iron Curtain speech.

On the other hand, most Western European states had a much more complex—not to say sophisticated—view of their relations with the Soviet Union. They were far more willing to appreciate that Soviet ambitions, whatever they might be, were more likely to be prosecuted by means that did not actually involve the use of Red Army forces. But there was a fundamental problem inherent in this difference in perspective on the two sides of the Atlantic: how could the west Europeans involve the United States in the destiny of the Continent, and particularly in its economic recovery, without also embracing the American view of the emerging Soviet 'threat'? It proved impossible to resolve this dilemma. Indeed, events made the dilemma worse. At every critical juncture, the American view of Soviet intentions seemed to be confirmed—first with the Prague *coup* of February 1948, then with the Berlin blockade, and finally with the Korean War in June 1950.

In the first instance, the Prague *coup* came at the end of a long chain of events. The Americans had proposed the Marshall Plan in June of 1947, a proposal for economic recovery in Europe that at first had even interested the Russians (Molotov came to the Paris Conference with a team of 70 aides). But then Moscow's interpretation of the American proposal shifted abruptly, and the Russians apparently came to view it as an imperialist venture—a comprehensible view perhaps, at a time of tension and misunderstanding. The Russians also required Poland and Czechoslovakia to withdraw from the Paris Conference, and the Marshall Plan became a purely Western venture, as the Americans preferred, anyway.

As a counter, later in 1947 Moscow instituted the Cominform, a restructuring of the old Comintern that had been disbanded as a mark of Allied solidarity during the war. From then on, a confrontation was approaching in economic and political terms. But it yet had to include a military element, since strong evidence was yet to come of a military threat in either direction.

It was not until after the failure of the London Foreign Ministers' Conference in December 1947 that the question of military force in the growing conflict came to the fore. But even then it was not inevitable that the Cold War should be seen in military terms, although the American view of Soviet intentions was swinging more and more behind this interpretation.

The turning point came with the proposal for a Western Union, made by the British Foreign Secretary, Ernest Bevin, in January 1948. This was an ambiguous proposal, that was designed at first to embrace five Western European nations— Britain, France, Belgium, the Netherlands and Luxembourg. Bevin was very unclear about the scope of his proposal, beyond its being a 'spiritual union'. He did not present it as a means of opposing the Soviet Union—except, in his words, 'to organize the kindred souls of the West'—nor did he single out one or another form of threat to Western European nations as being of central importance. As a result, the proposal was seen as all things to all men. In Britain and on the Continent, governments placed emphasis upon the political and economic aspects of the Western Union, in line with the prevailing interpretation of threat to Western European countries, which, as already noted, was seen in terms of subversion and economic weakness. In addition the continental nations saw the Western Union as the starting point for a process of encompassing political integration which, in so far as it would respond to any threat at all, looked towards Germany instead of towards the Soviet Union.

It was only in the United States that the Western Union proposal was welcomed for its military possibilities, as well. And here was the dilemma. Should the Europeans accept the American view of the purposes of this new venture—which included defence—or should they organize themselves solely according to their own lights and perhaps risk a new period of American isolationism towards Europe? This was not an idle question, since at stake was the whole structure—meaning the money—of the Marshall Plan, then stalled in Congress. It can be argued that the major reason for the timing of Bevin's Western Union proposal centred around the need to meet the demands of the American Congress and the Administration that Europeans show some incentive for self-help and self-organization. Those demands the Western Union seemed to meet, and the proposal was received as such in Washington.

But there were two difficulties with this development if the Western nations were to prevent the Cold War from being set in concrete. In the first place, the formation of an actual *bloc* in Western Europe, especially one that so clearly pleased the Americans, could only reduce the ambiguities that then existed in European politics about the division of Russian and American interests. As argued earlier, this reduction of ambiguity would be of some aid to many countries facing uncertainty about their future and about the terms of any debate or bargaining with the Soviet Union on vital questions such as the future of Germany and Austria.

But for other countries, there was less advantage to be found in this process—in particular, this included the countries where domination by Russia or America had not yet been confirmed: namely Finland, Austria, Poland and Czechoslovakia. In each of these countries, there was grave foreboding that the proposal for a Western Union would lead the Soviet Union to infer a greater threat to its security.

This may help to explain what happened next. For only a month after the promulgation of the Western Union, the regime in Prague was overturned by a *coup*—a *coup* that was widely taken in the West as the signal of a new phase in Soviet behaviour. But the flurry of anxiety that followed this event is hard to comprehend outside of the context of the times. After all, the *coup* had been widely predicted, as the result of the Western move towards crystallizing the division of Europe, and it actually moved no territory across the implicit strategic 'line', which was established at the end of the Second World War, but which had been little more than a psychological barrier until 1948. It may be argued that the Russians were over-reacting (just as they over-reacted in August 1968) and that, in turn, the Western nations over-reacted as well.

In any event, the Czech *coup* seemed to prove the Americans right: that there was, indeed, a military threat to Western Europe and that military preparations had to be taken to counter it. As a result, the treaty signed among the five Western Union powers took on a predominantly military character, although it still retained important elements of political and economic co-operation (see Appendix I). These latter elements are usually neglected in histories of this period. The reasons for that—as well as the significance of these developments—are discussed in Chapter 5.

The Prague *coup* gave the emerging Cold War a major push towards its military phase. But even then the Europeans were not as convinced as were the Americans of the military nature

of the Soviet threat, for they did very little to prepare themselves against it in the year that led up to the signature of the
North Atlantic Treaty. For them, the military threat was still
seen to be of secondary importance, if it existed at all.

Indeed, the next major Soviet move was also sufficiently
ambiguous to permit differences of interpretation in the West.
The Berlin blockade seemed to prove the Americans right by
showing once again that the Russians were prepared to use
military force to gain some advantage in the uncertain areas of
central Europe. It is still not clear that this was so, or that a
show of military force by the West—however small—would not
have broken the blockade there and then.

But whatever the Russians' intentions at this point, the fact
that the blockade of 1948–49 was broken without the use of
military force raises the question if this event should be interpreted as a military (as well as political) manoeuvre. Whether
this argument is valid or not, the Americans were given the
'evidence' they needed to convince reluctant European statesmen.
Indeed, the negotiations to create a North Atlantic Alliance
were conducted in the context of the blockade, and culminated
in a treaty whose non-military aspects were of minor importance from the point of view of the United States, although this
opinion was not shared by all West Europeans (see Appendix II).

Even then, there continued to be a divergence of opinion
about the actual nature of the Soviet threat. In France, for
example, there has never been more than a bare majority of
public opinion willing to believe in a Soviet military threat to
Western Europe. Furthermore, in virtually every European
member country of NATO at the time it was created, this new
treaty was seen more as a diplomatic venture—an American
guarantee with little that was tangible to back it up—than as
the formation of a full-scale and viable military alliance.
Indeed, the first year of NATO followed the pattern of development of the Brussels Treaty Organization (Western Union
Defence Organization); there was a striking lack of any real
acceptance of a military threat to Western Europe. The signing

of the North Atlantic Treaty was followed by, even if it did not cause, the ending of the Berlin blockade. Surely, it was argued in Europe, this proved that a diplomatic show of strength was sufficient to give the Western Europeans enough psychological confidence to allow them to put into effect the far more important Marshall Plan for economic recovery?

But once again, it was an external event—and one that did not necessarily imply an impending Soviet attack on Western Europe—that turned the tables. In June 1950, North Korea attacked her southern neighbour, in what appeared to be a war of aggression sponsored by the Soviet Union. In Western Europe, the Americans presented their view that this was part of a general Soviet expansionist effort—only a feint perhaps— and the whole idea of a military threat to Western Europe gained more currency than before. It was enough, anyway, to lead to the formation of an actual organization for NATO— the Allied Command Europe—within which the Americans agreed to supplement their meagre garrison forces with four divisions plus General Eisenhower, in exchange for real efforts by the Europeans to build up forces on their own. Thus there came into being within the context of NATO a real military presence on the ground; and this was the final act of militarizing the Cold War, almost exactly two years after the North Atlantic Treaty was signed.

Even then, the panic caused by the Korean War did not last very long. Within months, the Europeans sank back into indifference concerning the possibility of a Russian military threat. It was in the autumn of 1951 that the first great NATO exercise began in which the Americans tried to get their European allies to take seriously the demands of defence—one of a series of such exercises that will be described in more detail in later chapters.

It can be seen, therefore, that three events—the Prague *coup*, the Berlin blockade, and the Korean War—hastened the development of military Cold War in Europe. But even then, the European appreciation of the Soviet 'threat' to Western

Europe was never as high as that held by the Americans, except in one country—West Germany. Indeed, it was only on the question of admitting it to NATO and beginning its rearmament that there developed significant European pressure towards emphasizing the importance of NATO's defences, and sufficient motivation by any of these countries to begin the repeated crises of confidence that surrounded the 'nuclear sharing' issues of the 1960s—to be described in Chapter 4. But these were issues that were more important in terms of possible West German diplomatic power and the relative importance within the alliance of the United States and its European allies, than issues connected with countering an actual military threat.

In Western Europe, perceptions of an actual military threat from the Soviet Union did rise somewhat in the late 1950s, during the period, 1958–61, of the so-called 'Berlin crises'. But even now it is unclear what the Russians were trying to achieve by exerting pressures on West Berlin: whether they actually harboured a motive for expansion, or were merely trying to take one political issue of the Cold War—the status of Berlin—from the realm of uncertainty into that of certainty. Whatever the Russian motivation, after the last crisis ended in 1961 with the building of the Berlin Wall, there ceased for all practical purposes to be any real strategic uncertainty anywhere in Europe and, partially as a result, there was a serious downgrading of appreciations of military threat to Western Europe, even as viewed from the United States. This was largely a psychological reaction: as long as there was some part of Europe whose status was not confirmed, there could possibly be seen a certain Soviet pressure to revise frontiers. But once that problem was finally settled—in particular, to prevent the further draining away of East German workers and to end the Soviet threats of a unilateral peace treaty with East Germany—there was no longer an issue that could be used as the focus for anxieties about European security.

From then onwards, there was a further intensification of what has been known as the problem of 'cohesion' within the

Alliance, a problem that had first arisen for almost the opposite reasons when the Russians acquired, some time between 1956 and 1960, an ability to attack the United States directly with nuclear weapons, and the Europeans were no longer sure that their security could be allowed to depend on promises by the United States to use nuclear weapons in Europe's defence. But after 1961 appreciations of the Soviet threat declined throughout NATO, and the willingness to take defence problems seriously decreased as well. But this process was not uniform: the Germans were the last to concede that the military threat was, indeed, going down, since they were on the 'front line' and were most concerned with political change in Europe rather than acceptance of the *status quo*.

Of course, this reduction in the appreciation of the Soviet military threat begged the question of whether objectively there had ever really been such a threat. But still the new appreciation helped to lay the ground-work for *détente*, along with three other factors of importance: first, the recognition of the strategic certainty of European division, a certainty that had really been present—except possibly in the case of Berlin—ever since West Germany entered NATO in 1955; second, the beginnings of American-Soviet strategic stability after the Cuban missile crisis of October 1962; and third, the growth of East-West intercourse in a large number of areas, particularly that of economics.

The French, of course, were the first to exploit the general appreciation of a reduction in the Soviet military threat. But they were not alone in having the potential to do so; other European nations could also have exploited the emerging *détente*, but apparently did not do so because they lacked the French inclination to place a higher value on gaining increased diplomatic flexibility than on retaining the marginal advantages that would be provided by ensuring a continued American military presence on the Continent and preserving the psychological worth—for security—of the NATO organization.

The most important thing to note about this French attitude was its sincerity, at least in its appreciation of the Soviet military threat. After all, by the mid-1960s, there was very little remaining evidence to support a thesis that the Russians would undertake a serious military venture against NATO, with the possible exception of limited aggression to obtain the flank regions either in northern Norway or the Turkish border areas; and even in these instances the general concern expressed in the North Atlantic Council about a possible Russian threat to these outlying nations was perhaps intended more to give them a feeling of participation in the Alliance, rather than to provide an objective view. Even with the Russian invasion of Czechoslovakia in the summer of 1968, there was surprisingly little willingness by any NATO nation to believe that there had been an increase in the Soviet military threat to Western Europe. The Soviet invasion could be seen as consistent with the strategic understandings, if not the political ones, that formed at least part of the basis of *détente*. The concern about possible Russian aggression against Western Europe, as expressed by the Supreme Allied Commander, Europe (General Lemnitzer), went almost unheeded throughout the rest of the Alliance.

Yet the North Atlantic Council did take some remedial action, as though the tangible military threat had increased, and the French Government even modified its independent stand somewhat to join with the other fourteen nations in a collective warning against further Soviet military action in areas implicitly including Jugoslavia—where such action really would change the strategic *status quo*. But this NATO reaction was less a renewed appreciation of a real threat to Western Europe—there were few open avowals of this—than an appreciation that the Soviet action undercut another basis of *détente*—namely, the increasing intercourse between East and West Europe. Greater efforts in the military field—of marginal significance, as it happened—would therefore be signals that *détente* in Europe could not proceed unless Soviet rule in Eastern Europe was modified. It may be argued that this was the same sort of use made of military responses to counter a non-military 'threat' that helped to change the Cold War confrontation in Europe from the political and economic realm to the military realm in the first place. In this case, however, there was little danger of actually transforming the terms of the confrontation as had been true 20 years before.

Thus, it can be seen that over a period of nearly 20 years the establishment of a military *bloc* in Western Europe—in confrontation with a Soviet military *bloc* that was first a series of bilateral treaties and was later enshrined in the Warsaw Pact—created a logic of its own, a military logic, that then had to be followed through to its own conclusion.

Perhaps the most striking feature of this logic was the long-standing debate within NATO about the difference between the Russians' military 'capabilities' and their 'intentions'. It is interesting to note that the Soviet Union maintained an overwhelming conventional military capability in Europe for several years before this was interpreted in the West to mean that Soviet leaders were necessarily prepared to attack westwards. It was only after the context of military confrontation was established—beginning with the Prague *coup* and the Brussels Treaty—that Russian forces-in-being came to be seen as a positive threat, whether or not the Russians intended to use them for purposes of aggression. It seems to be a general principle, therefore, that as long as there is no context of conflict, then forces in being can be explained in many ways. But as soon as that context develops, in this case almost by accident or at least in part by a process of mutual misperception, then the internal logic of conflict requires that the numbers of forces should be seen to represent the nature of the threat. At least this was the way in which the Americans always saw the problem of Soviet forces in Eastern Europe, since, of course, it was they who were most directly locked into the context of conflict by being in direct confrontation with the Russians.

Beginning with the point at which the conflict was accepted in the West as one of a military nature (again, here is the process of 'selling' the American conception), then there was no alternative but to accept the logic of numbers, and prepare to counter the apparent threat of capabilities-equals-intentions. Only when something like a balance had been achieved in numbers of forces on each side of the division could there again be any rational thought upon the problem. Such a balance was achieved very early on in NATO's history when one added nuclear weapons—the panoply of deterrence—to the equation. But subsequently something like an actual parity of conventional forces was achieved in the late 1960s, as well, although this development has been hotly debated in the NATO Alliance, and depends in part on definitions of the time a war would remain 'conventional'. It is interesting to note that it is the Americans, trying to stimulate a slightly greater European military effort, who have seen parity as between NATO and Warsaw Pact forces, and the Europeans, led by the British Defence Secretary in 1969, who have disputed the American case and emphasized NATO's continuing reliance on American nuclear arms.

It is no coincidence that, as perceived tensions decreased, NATO intelligence experts (led by the United States, which was by then most anxious for a relaxation of tensions and a bilateral *détente* with the Soviet Union) saw that earlier estimates of Russian troop strengths (the famous 175 divisions) had been exaggerated. They had been exaggerated, so the argument ran, not just immediately before the new appreciation, but from the start. Therefore, by the early 1960s, it was possible for some NATO countries to begin to see a decreasing disparity in conventional weapon and force levels between the two Alliances that would allow some distinction to be made between Russian intentions and capabilities. The process of dissociating the two factors took some time longer; it was not until December 1967 that, after further intelligence down-grading of Soviet forces, the North Atlantic Council accepted formally the distinction between the Soviets' military force levels and their political intentions. This change was, of course, facilitated by other moves towards *détente*. But it does illustrate the internal demands of a logic of military confrontation, and is a commentary on the high price paid for security by all countries in Europe, East and West, for their failure to find a basis for bargaining without engaging in a costly and dangerous military confrontation. Interestingly enough, the Soviet invasion of Czechoslovakia did not mean more than a partial reversion to the old identification of capabilities and intentions in NATO's view of Soviet behaviour—although the Supreme Allied Commander Europe pressed for such a reversion to it, as he always had done. And this testifies to the way in which the subtleties of politics can survive, once the original internal logic of military confrontation has been worked out, and then set in train a process of relaxed and rational thought about the whole context and process of diplomatic, economic, political and military conflict.

A similar process was, of course, taking place on the Soviet side—or so at least one can presume. Relaxation in tensions perceived on that side also came at a time when the Western military preponderance—in this case denominated in nuclear weapons and the relative invulnerability of the United States—was disappearing. Here, however, the Russians seem to have been more impressed, not by their new ability to deter the United States with nuclear weapons, but rather by the decrease of anxieties felt by the Western nations and, as a result, a decrease in the latter's emphasis upon the conflict aspects of East-West relations. Numbers of forces and weapons had always mattered less for the Russians than had their appreciation of Western intentions as viewed from outside the context of the arms balance; now the West seemed to be sharing that view while the Russians, in turn, began to see that, up to a point, numbers and types of weapons are relevant to providing strategic stability.

For years, the Russians had been concerned about Western intentions towards them—a 'threat'—but this had been less the fear of specific levels of weapons and forces, including nuclear weapons, than the observation that a context of conflict did exist. The Russians could see that there were outstanding political issues in contention—beginning with the political organization of Eastern Europe in 1944 and dominated through-out by the twin problems of Germany and Berlin. But for the Russians it was these issues, and not the mere existence of weapons, that mattered. In a way, the Western view of Soviet force levels in Eastern Europe before a political context of conflict was created in 1947–8 characterized the Soviet view of Western armaments throughout the Cold War period. These Western armaments were seen by the Russians primarily as adjuncts to the underlying political conflict, rarely, as in the West from at least 1955–62, as establishing an environment of their own that had first to be stabilized, without reference to East-West political relations, before the 'logic' of Cold War could come to an end.

This may seem to be almost a chicken-and-egg problem, but it is not quite that. To set in motion the process of transition from a time of threat to one of *détente*, the Western nations had first to feel the security of *numbers* that would start the process of relaxation—the change in context—to which the Russians could then respond. This is not to say that the Russians were not always very wary of the 'numbers game'—they were surely sufficiently influenced by American atomic bombs in the late 1940s to be even more mistrustful of American actions (a tendency reinforced, of course, by Marxist ideology, just as American anti-Communism reinforced American mistrust of the Russians).

But given the philosophical differences between America and Russia about the pre-eminence of weapons in a context of confrontation, as opposed to the nature of the interests involved in the confrontation itself, it was natural that America should be first to define that the Cold War had entered a necessarily military phase (at about the time of the Prague *coup*). And it was natural that they should be first to define that it had come out of that phase (after the Cuban missile crisis).

Such was the nature of the 'threat' as it was perceived on either side during the years of NATO's formation and develop-ment. But perception of threat did more than just bring into being two military *blocs* in confrontation with one another; it led to the creation of an elaborate diplomatic network in East and West that radically transformed the nature of relations between many states. Some of these problems—particularly those arising out of the internal organization of NATO—will be the subject of the next chapter.

Chapter 3

The Role of Institutions

When the North Atlantic Treaty was signed and ratified by the twelve governments in 1949, it was still necessary to transform a diplomatic instrument into a firm set of institutions.[1] As mentioned in the last chapter, this process did not begin immediately, nor was it concluded on a straightforward and ordered basis. Instead, the institutions of the Alliance—the 'O' in NATO—grew up piecemeal as more and more statesmen came to see the diplomatic guarantees as inadequate. But a context of conflict was coming clearly into focus. In order to make that context concrete—that is, in order to follow through the logic of military confrontation—it was necessary to create institutional structures that would represent firm evidence of Western intentions, particularly those of the United States. And these intentions had to be clear both to the potential enemy and to all the Allies.

For the first year, little was done to create an actual organization. The twelve member states managed to constitute themselves into a Council, composed of their foreign ministers, and to provide also for councils including their defence and finance ministers. Beyond that, they did little of value except to begin half-hearted attempts to co-ordinate their meagre defence efforts. Five Regional Planning Groups were set up—one, significantly, embracing intact the entire Western Union Defence Organization of Britain, France and the Benelux states—but there was no prospect that this collection of planning groups would ever prosecute a war, or even respond with any measure of success to an attack. There was, in short, no practical means of implementing the guarantees spelt out in the North

---

[1] Greece and Turkey joined in 1952; West Germany joined in 1955.

Atlantic Treaty to the effect that each nation would regard an attack on any other as an attack on itself.

The only real guarantee was one given by the Americans to their new allies. And, for the time being, that was enough: the American assurances had some psychological value, and there was the vague spectre of an American atomic arsenal, although it was of precious small dimensions, that gave some meaning to the military aspects of the newly structured East-West confrontation in Europe.

But with the beginning of the Korean War the contradictions posed by having a military confrontation without any really effective military potential became more apparent or at least, as noted earlier, the Americans found that they could present this case with more assurance of finding a sympathetic audience in Western Europe.

In this way the first real elements of military power actually to be concentrated and directed within the NATO organization were brought into being. In late 1950, the United States agreed to place four divisions in a supranational command that would be headed by General Dwight D. Eisenhower, a folk-hero in Europe and the first of a succession of Supreme Allied Commanders, Europe, all of whom have been American generals. This Allied Command Europe was charged with implementing what has become famous as the 'forward strategy'—the intention of defending Western Europe, should there ever be an attack from the East, as far 'forward' as possible. This was no more than sound military thinking. But for those states lying just to the west of Germany, this forward strategy had a particular meaning: if it was to be at all relevant, it had to prevent the fighting from taking place on their own soil. And this meant, quite simply, that there would have to be some form of defence of West Germany itself.

Therefore, the very act of formulating a strategy for NATO compromised the already complex quality of the West German government which had been formed in 1949. In its attempt to make its strategic doctrines as rational and sensible as possible

—however implausible it might have been to try mounting an actual defence—the Alliance had arranged to include West Germany within its ambit. In other words, any further value that might be derived from continued ambiguity about the status of Germany in the context of East-West relations—in order to facilitate, for example, a resolution of conflicts over Germany at some future date—was virtually lost. But it was not entirely lost even then: after all, the Russians did not settle down to take a consistent line on West Germany until 1955 after the conclusion of the Western European Union agreements and Germany's entry into NATO. In the intervening years the Russians demonstrated their flexibility on German questions in acts such as their flamboyant gesture in March 1954 of actually suggesting that they might join NATO! But when West Germany became a formal part of the Western Alliance, the Russians then sought to formalize the permanent division of Germany in the process of organizing the Warsaw Pact.

In any event, the logic of the forward strategy quickly made itself felt: if West Germany were to be included in the defence, then there would surely have to be a great quantity of soldiers and equipment available, and what better place to find them than in Germany itself? This was anyway the logic pursued by the Americans. Therefore, as early as late 1950, the decision to rearm Germany was taken in principle by the North Atlantic Council. This was an important event, for it not only signalled an effort by the Americans to allay fears about German revanchism on the part of the European allies—at least sufficiently to get troops provided for the forward strategy. It also began four years of bitter wrangling about the most appropriate means for bringing West Germany back into the comity of nations—that is, to secure the use of German troops. And, of course, once the Germans started actually to provide troops, the United States—as well as the Soviet Union—would have to think clearly about giving all sorts of guarantees—tacit or explicit—to those countries both in Eastern and Western Europe that saw in the Federal Republic of Germany a greater threat to their security than they saw in either of the two super-powers. More than that, once these German troops were involved, the Russians could no longer give anybody the benefit of the doubt about the status of West Germany—though, of course, the Russians had started the process off by equipping the East Germans with a small force of *Kasinierte Volkspolizei*, by any other name an army. NATO's decision to rearm West Germany was, therefore, a signal act, not only in the context of relations inside NATO (it was the genesis of almost two decades of 'German problem' within the Alliance), but also in the context of finding ground for accommodation with the Soviet Union. It was just one more difficulty, and a central one. Of course, one might argue that clarifying the position of the two Germanies would help to bring on a period of strategic stability on the Continent that was one requirement of *détente*, but this is an historical point that is impossible to judge adequately.

In order to meet American arguments, the NATO Allies in the autumn of 1950 agreed to the raising of German forces, and at the end of 1954 a method to do this was accomplished. In the process, there developed an ambitious venture in European integration, the European Defence Community; then the EDC was defeated in the French Chamber of Deputies; and finally the British Government brought into effect a splendid diplomatic *coup de main* in proposing Western European Union. The British thereby found a way of creating German forces, while at the same time remaining aloof from direct political involvement in Continental affairs, appearing to be a good and loyal NATO ally, and preserving their chances of a 'special relationship' with the United States (see Chapter 5).

With the prospect that NATO forces actually would be raised, Allied Command Europe sprang into being on April 1st, 1951. NATO had finally become an organization (see Appendix VI). Its Supreme Headquarters, Allied Powers Europe (SHAPE) were in temporary buildings in a suburb of Paris, where they remained for exactly 16 years, until asked to retire by General de Gaulle. This proved the adage that flourishing institutions can make do with just about any kind of real property: it is only those institutions that are dying that have the time to build palaces.

The problems facing the new Supreme Allied Commander Europe (known universally by the acronym SACEUR) were formidable, as were the problems facing the civilian side of the Alliance. No one had ever done anything like this before—at least not in peace time. This was a grand coalition of twelve sovereign nations, each pledged to the defence of all. And the coalition included the unprecedented 'integrated' military command—although no one has ever quite understood the meaning of the word 'integrated'.

In these early days of NATO there were trials and errors, on both the civilian and military sides of the Alliance. But for every problem a committee was created, so that by late 1951, it was hard to see the institution for the committees of which it was composed. This was a not unnatural development, and reflected, if anything, the massive problems of operating such an enormous enterprise with nations which had only two basic interests in common: first, to maintain whatever defence should from time to time be thought necessary—particularly when the Americans were successful in presenting their view of the threat —and second, to keep the United States firmly committed to the Continent, both strategically and for the purposes of economic and military aid. And with only slight modification, primarily in the financial arrangements, these are still the only real objectives binding the nations of the Alliance together, although, as discussed in Chapter 5, there have been many attempts to broaden the mandate of the organization.

But gradually some sense began to be made of the problems of NATO's organization. On the civilian side, three separate councils of ministers—foreign affairs, defence, finance—were consolidated into a single council, where the appropriate ministers could meet from time to time. Then the whole civilian side of the Alliance was moved from London to Paris, and a permanent staff was slowly evolved, first through a body called the Council Deputies, and then through the creation of a permanent Staff/Secretariat. This latter body was headed from 1952–57 by the able Scot, Lord Ismay, and thereafter by a succession of lesser lights.

The problems of running the civilian side of the Alliance have never been rationalized to anyone's real satisfaction. But there were some terrible handicaps. First, to preserve the appearance of unity within the Alliance, the North Atlantic Council has always effectively taken decisions by unanimous vote. This is a clue in itself to the relative ineffectiveness of this body, and to the limited aims of the Alliance generally. As experience with the League of Nations showed, there had to be some disproportionate weight in voting for more important powers if anything was to be accomplished through this mechanism. Hence the voting procedures in the UN Security Council— a good conception, even if it assumed too much common interest among the five permanent members. So too, the European Economic Community adopted a system of weighted voting within its Council of Ministers that extended progressively to cover more important business, although it has rarely been used; in practice, unanimity is still the rule where any matter of real importance is at issue.

But this approach did not apply to the North Atlantic Council, unfortunately perhaps, for not only did this procedure of 'effective unanimity' maintain a fiction of equality amongst the member states—a fiction that later helped to reinforce resentment of American domination of the Alliance; it also meant a greater need to arrive at decisions around a lowest common denominator, a point that, as often as not, involved some concept of the indivisibility of the Cold War. And this in turn meant that it has been difficult to consider accommodation with the Soviet Union at any one particular point. Thus the context of conflict in Europe was reinforced by the manner in which the North Atlantic Council was organized—though perhaps this was not too high a price to pay in exchange for having a viable Alliance at all. In addition, the pattern of taking decisions in the Council, often only a process of ratifying decisions concluded through informal caucus or bilateral bargaining between the United States and other countries, may have actually delayed the end of the Cold War by inhibiting individual nations from exploiting potential understandings about the political and strategic *status quo*.

In the early years, it may be safely said that the civilian side of the North Atlantic Treaty Organization was a means for the United States to exert its influence on its various Allies; to formulate ways of allocating the costs of the Alliance between nations; to put pressure on nations to meet their economic and military commitments; and to give a sense of unity and solidarity to the Alliance that did give NATO a certain élan. As time went on, however, the pattern of American domination became less acceptable to some of the European members of the Alliance, which members then tried to redress the balance. Unfortunately, the format of unity in the North Atlantic Council, among other factors, inhibited the making of changes—as when the French, in 1958, proposed that responsibility for general Western interests, not just those within the NATO area, be divided among America, Britain and France. The proposal was received with coolness in Washington.

Among the first tasks to be faced by the North Atlantic Council—one which it has had to face ever since—was the matter of raising funds with which to operate and, of course, of raising troops to implement the forward strategy. How was the burden to be shared? Or, at the very worst, how was American aid to be apportioned among the various Allies who were to receive help under the Mutual Defence Assistance Programme? After a few false starts, the Council in the autumn of 1951 appointed a Temporary Council Committee to look into the matter, and decide upon a doctrine of 'fair shares' for each of the member countries. What this committee bargained out was later adopted as the famous Lisbon force goals of February 1952 —so named because of the location of the relevant Council meeting. These goals were indeed ambitious—some 96 divisions by 1954, including 25 to 30 divisions in battle readiness to be stationed on the Central Front in central Europe.

Immediately, a 'numbers game' began, with the 96 divisions serving as a shibboleth of loyalty to the Alliance and to the NATO 'concept'. For years, various NATO Allies were berated for not keeping up their quotas, and the whole Alliance was often said to be militarily vulnerable for not having met the force goals. In fact, of course, there was no Soviet attack throughout that time, so the missing divisions could not have been all that important, except psychologically. In addition, as long as these divisions were missing, it was hard to think of the NATO Alliance as being the military equal of the Soviet Union or, therefore, of there being any abatement of the 'threat'. Thus the Cold War was even further prolonged.

In fact, the Central Front force goals of 25 to 30 divisions—whatever they meant in terms of a viable strategy—were virtually attained by the early 1960s. But there were still few countries that actually met their agreed quotas, particularly when reserve requirements were taken into account. This failure occurred for a variety of reasons, chief among which must be accorded the differing perceptions of the actual Soviet threat among the Allies. It was one thing to accept the American concept of the Soviet threat almost by default; it was quite another to back this concept with money and men, particularly when several European countries had originally thought they were merely bargaining to gain some American protection that would free economic resources for reconstruction and, later on, for economic development.

There were other reasons as well, including an important strategic one that will be explored on its own in Chapter 4. And there was involved a process of bargaining among the various Allies—not just a common effort to solve common problems but more an attempt by each Ally to see which other countries could be induced to carry a greater weight of its own burden. Throughout this process of bargaining that extended over the whole life of the Alliance—particularly bargaining by European nations that attempted to shift the major part of the burden on to the United States—there was a series of attempts to arrive at so-called 'objective' standards for determining relative effort. The standard cited most commonly in the context of the so-called 'Annual Review' has been that of the percentage of each nation's gross national product devoted to defence. But this standard has never been particularly meaningful, and it has impressed few statesmen. After all, there was no corresponding concept of the different returns in terms of security gained by each country. Certainly some countries had more to gain from the existence of NATO than did others—the extremes perhaps being West Germany and Canada. Nor was there any attempt within NATO to reach an 'objective' standard of the political influence gained by various nations within the Alliance. The United States, for example, gained overwhelming influence within NATO, probably even more than would be proportional to the relative size of the United States' GNP or its dollar contribution to the Alliance as a whole.

Ever since the Lisbon force goals, however, there has been a regular succession of efforts to induce various countries to live up to their force commitments. At the same time, there have been efforts to revise and adapt these commitments to differing notions of 'realism'—both with regard to the threat and concerning the best strategy for the Alliance. This has been a process of political bargaining and is all the more interesting for that. But if ever one desires evidence that NATO has been, first, last, and always, only a loose coalition of nations with limited common interests, this bargaining process is the place to look.

In the mid-1960s, the Americans led an attempt to meet this problem in its own terms and to accept that planning for military purposes should be made on the basis of the forces actually made available by member countries, rather than on the mythical goals that everyone knew would never be attained. This was a rational compromise, but it did not last long, before the same old appeals were being renewed for individual states to increase their force contributions. This was a matter that reflected a changing concept of NATO strategy, and will be discussed further in Chapter 4.

There was also an important problem in the development of NATO that centred on financial questions. This may seem a peripheral topic, but it was really at the heart of the NATO Alliance and related in particular to the gradual evolution of American dominance and to the increasing reactions against this dominance.

Particularly interesting was the process, begun in the mid-1960s, in which the Federal German Republic agreed to make available funds to offset the drain on the balance of payments of the United States and the United Kingdom, owing to military forces stationed in West Germany. This process was all right as far as it went—after all, the West Germans were gaining a good deal of foreign exchange as well as security through the presence of American and British forces. In addition, the distribution of political influence within the Alliance enabled Washington and London to extract significant amounts of money from a West German government which saw these offset payments as premiums on insurance against a future withdrawal of American and British forces from the Continent, while the United States and Britain received help to meet their growing balance of payments difficulties.

The Americans did particularly well, gaining an agreement from the West Germans in 1965 to make offset payments, in one form or another, totalling $1,300 million over a two-year period. Unfortunately, however, the offset talks became a regular feature of NATO activities, and at times seemed to be more important to the Anglo-Saxon Allies than more political or military features of the Alliance. Another such agreement was concluded in 1967, in which the United States agreed to help Britain economically, while West Germany would take steps to ease the balance of payments problems of both.

This effort illustrated many things: and among them was evidence of the close relationship between the economic

44

strength of the various NATO partners and the bargaining process that went on within the Alliance. Ironically, it was the consistently undervalued West German mark—denominated at a figure arbitrarily set in 1949—that produced patterns of negotiation within NATO that had implications for the way in which other powers looked at the organization's potential as a forum for considering political problems that went beyond the provision of security. This was so because the bargaining on offset costs was conducted on a strictly tripartite basis. Although the other Allies were kept informed, this bargaining process dramatized the fact that, in practice, only three nations were taking decisions affecting all the Allies, as did the offset agreements of 1967 which entailed the 'redeployment' of US and UK military units back to their home bases, away from the Continent. And a similar judgement can be made concerning the economic factors that helped lead the Allies to accept a modification of NATO's strategy in 1967 (see Chapter 4).

This process, therefore, helped to isolate further the other Allies from negotiations about the basic interests of the Alliance. This was a further indication that, when basic interests of the great powers were involved, the formal 15-nation structure of the Alliance would be conveniently by-passed, especially by the United States; and it was an indication that the West Germans were gaining an ever-increasing importance within the Alliance. There was some logic for this offset-cost procedure. After all, other European allies were benefiting less than the West Germans in terms of foreign exchange from having US and British troops on the Continent. But there seemed to be little understanding in this reasoning that those other nations were benefiting significantly in the more fundamental terms of *security*. The Germans alone were saddled with responsibility for helping out the British and American balance of payments and, as part of this process, effectively gained a greater say in making NATO policies—a development that would be especially important when and if it would be time to worry about the priorities to be adopted in seeking a resolution of the division of Europe and the division of Germany.

This lesson was not lost on General de Gaulle: at no time did he ask the West Germans for a single franc to offset support costs for the two French divisions that remained in the Federal Republic. This policy both tended to strengthen his hand in Bonn, and to keep him from becoming at all dependent on the West German Economics Minister. This was a policy he also seemed to be pursuing in November 1968, during the crisis over the weakness of the franc, when he ruled out devaluation even though the West Germans would not revalue the mark. Only in 1969 did the Allies as a whole take account of this problem of offset payments and influence within the Alliance, though without specifically recognizing the problem as such, when the debate was partially shifted from the question of foreign exchange—a trilateral concern of the British, Americans and Germans—to the question of actual budgetary support for those countries supplying forces, a matter that could more logically include all the Allies.

On the civilian side of the NATO Alliance, discussions often came back down to the question of money. And this was, in turn, a shorthand method of computing the distribution of influence within the Alliance—insofar as anything as intangible as 'influence' can be measured—according to a standard of willingness and ability to pay. It was a bargaining process, with no real sense of 'fair shares', except to the extent that a particular nation could arrive, through negotiations, at a higher or lower figure for its contribution. All the Allies were involved in this process of settling on influence; and, therefore, when these crucial issues were taken out of a 15-nation context and placed in a three-nation context, the 'institutional myth' of NATO as a consortium of 'equal' powers wore a bit thin— again, a matter of more importance to the future of joint NATO efforts to resolve the Cold War divisions.

Of course, there had always been a central weakness inherent in a process of bargaining for influence through the mechanism of contributions made to the Alliance: political 'influence' tends to be distributed on a scale according to quantum jumps rather than on a continuum. Thus, a small power in NATO that was contributing—say—1/20th of the American share of the 'common defence', would only be able to exercise perhaps 1/1000th (if that) of the total political influence in the Alliance. It was very much like America's being a stockholder with a controlling interest of the shares: smaller holdings did not necessarily buy proportionate influence. This situation did not always benefit the Americans, however: it may help to explain why the Alliance never seemed to be able to meet its force goals, with the smaller nations often lagging farther behind the others. It was one thing for the US to have influence for such purposes as arriving at a common strategy or common appreciation of 'threat'; it was quite another to use that influence to stimulate positive efforts to provide money or troops on the part of governments that would not gain proportionate influence for their efforts.

But for all the efforts made on the civilian side of NATO, this has really been a secondary part of the Alliance. There have been semi-annual meetings of foreign and defence ministers. But these have paled beside the continuing influence of the military structure of the Alliance, particularly of Allied Command Europe, an institution which actually has had forces on permanent station, forces that would, in effect at least, respond to the commands of the integrated commander, SACEUR.

Yet first and foremost, SACEUR has been a diplomat. And as such he has faced a number of peculiar problems. In particular, he has always been an American officer, partly because of the predominant role that America has played throughout in the Alliance and—after the mid-1950s—partly because of the need to have as commander the only man who could take the necessary order from the American President to use the nuclear weapons in NATO's arsenal. SACEUR has also been the commander of US forces in Europe, and of the US 7th Army.

He wears, as the Pentagon would phrase it, 'three hats'. Which one he 'wears' at any one time depends upon his function at the moment, the temper of the man, and the pressures he is under to conform to the wishes of Washington.

General Eisenhower was, first and foremost, the best man alive to make appeals to various European countries on matters of contributing forces and money. He did the job as well as any man could, which was moderately well. Whatever skills as a military commander he might have possessed in addition to his diplomatic skills were more or less an unexpected bonus.

The second SACEUR seemed to prove the widely accepted rule about diplomats and politicians who are really military men in training and temperament. General Ridgway was an excellent battlefield commander; but he was a disaster as SACEUR, because he never seemed to understand the rigorous political and diplomatic demands placed on him in this job— as the only man who was in a position to perform the essential function of prising money and men out of 14 nations, including the new Allies, Greece and Turkey. But the next SACEUR, General Gruenther, improved on his predecessor's record: he had, after all, followed the development of NATO as an institution since its beginning and knew the demands placed upon the symbolic leader of the Alliance.

But the most extraordinary SACEUR of all was one of America's most extraordinary officers, General Lauris Norstad. It was clear which 'hat' he preferred to wear: that of the European presiding over a coalition of states. Indeed, he came so well to reflect the needs and demands of the NATO organization itself—the 'compleat' organization man and a superb politician—that during his tenure the grip of the United States on the Alliance was weakened, and NATO enjoyed its finest hours as a coalition where political problems could also be tentatively advanced, instead of being confined to external bilateral forums. Regrettably, General Norstad's independence from Washington did not go down well with President Kennedy or Mr McNamara, his Secretary of Defense, and Norstad was recalled in 1961, to be replaced by General Lyman Lemnitzer, a man of lesser political skills and independence of mind and temperament. Since then, the relations of the United States with various alliance members have never been the same, and the problems of reconciling American and collective European interests have increased significantly, though of course for a complex of reasons of which this has been only one, however important.

There is no doubt that SACEUR has been the pre-eminent official in NATO throughout the years since 1951. Other commanders, whatever their nationality, could never compete with him for authority and influence, either within the American Government or within Allied circles. There were, indeed, other commands: one for the English Channel, which has never had much reality; and one for the Atlantic, with its Headquarters in Norfolk, Virginia, and which has been based largely upon the preponderance of American seapower. As such, Allied Command Atlantic has had even less scope as a forum for Allied consultation and for the bargaining of matters related to the distribution of political influence within the Alliance. In addition, in this command—as in SACEUR's subordinate Mediterranean command, consisting primarily of the US Sixth Fleet—forces have only been 'earmarked'—i.e. set aside in readiness—for use by international commanders in time of crisis or of yearly exercises, whereas the forces of Allied Command Europe have actually been 'assigned' to SACEUR and effectively operate under his general command. Individual nations with forces in Allied Command Europe still retain, in theory, the right to decide whether or not to commit their forces to battle. But the tenuous lines of communication maintained between SHAPE and home capitals (except to the capitals of the principal powers, especially Washington) as well as the difficulties that would be posed by attempts actually to withdraw forces under fire, make this technicality more or less meaningless. Indeed, this was one of the reasons that led the French Government to remove its forces from Allied Command

Europe in 1966: in order to give Paris a better chance to decide whether to join in battle. This was, of course, a largely diplomatic exercise, since French ground forces were stationed well back in Germany against the French border, and would not have been engaged in any initial Soviet attack anyway. On the other hand, French air squadrons would have been involved, come what may, and were accordingly withdrawn from Germany, although for purposes of NATO air *defence*, the French continued to avail themselves of the common system.

This role of the Supreme Allied Commander, Europe, was pre-eminent, but this was true only in practice. In theory, he was for most of SHAPE's first 18 years subject to the authority of one of the myriad NATO bodies—actually there were only 291 of them in 1967—the so-called Standing Group of the Military Committee. This small body consisted of the representatives of the Chiefs of Staff of Britain, France and the United States, and was actually stationed in Washington in silent testimony to the dominant role played by the United States. It was technically only a permanent embodiment of the Military Committee, a body which nominally included all the Allies but which effectively had little importance. And even the Standing Group, as the 'superior body responsible for the highest strategic guidance' in the Alliance, was a body of little significance: it ratified the recommendations sent to it by SACEUR and sent them back as their instructions to him. Even the American government preferred dealing through the clear and direct lines to SACEUR, sometimes to the disgust of the two other members of the Standing Group, especially France. Not without justification, the French long believed that the United States was arrogating to itself more influence than even its great economic and military importance warranted. Indeed, a proposal made by France in 1958 for the creation of a triumvirate of France, Britain and America to direct all Western activity in the world was designed in part to clarify the ambiguous nature of the Standing Group, and to expose its rule, not as hypocrisy, perhaps, but at least as a casualty of the failure of European states to find some means of countering American dominance.

In 1967, as part of the reorganization of NATO which followed on the 'defection' of France, the Standing Group was abolished: this was an act which was symbolically important as a means of chastising the French for not 'playing the game', but which had no military significance. Instead, there was an effort to 'rationalize' the structure of the Alliance; policy direction for SACEUR now came straight from the Military Committee effectively composed of 14 nations. This arrangement, of course, was no more meaningful than having the Standing Group, and it made it even less likely that there would be any formal, institutional means for representing at SHAPE the very real differences of influence available to the different member states. In terms of institutional programming, the change might have looked like an attempt to produce greater efficiency, but in practical terms it did little if anything to change the pattern of America's domination of the Alliance.

The institutional arrangements of NATO have also served functions different from the formal ones accorded to them, either by the Treaty itself or by later agreements. They have, in particular, helped to bring about a greater willingness among various of the Allied nations to focus attention on their relations with one another, in many cases concentrating attention that would otherwise have been directed towards problems elsewhere in the world. NATO certainly added to the sense of security in Western Europe within which context the relations of these Allied states were further developed—including such ventures as the European Economic Community. This was a very important and complicated process and it will be described in some detail in Chapter 5. Furthermore the institutions of NATO certainly have given the Americans—as the dominant partner—the opportunity to decide when to deal with their Allies on a bilateral basis, and when to use the forums of NATO for particular purposes, such as applying collective moral pressures to secure financial and troop commitments to the Alliance.

And NATO's institutions certainly have given the West Germans a greater feeling of participation than they could possibly have attained outside the Alliance. Indeed, this was a conscious policy adopted by the Federal German Chancellor, Dr Adenauer, who postponed any active policy designed to secure reunification of Germany in order to gain respectability and purpose through involvement in NATO. This policy certainly succeeded, although one might argue that the close involvement of West Germany in the affairs of Western defence actually deferred the time when the Russians and Americans could consider once again the thorny question of the future of Germany.

But diplomatically—and symbolically—West Germany has certainly played its part in NATO organs, gaining from this a sense of participation which was essential to what was widely seen as the re-establishment of an idea of national worth. There have been German officers occupying high positions in the military commands—rising to the level of Commander of Allied Forces, Central Europe. And throughout the NATO organization, West Germans have taken their place in a series of military and civilian institutions which were notable for their role in promoting co-operation at the 'working levels' among nations that had relatively little in common beyond the basic goals of the Alliance. Indeed, when General de Gaulle withdrew his contingents from Allied Command Europe and requested the departure of all NATO military commands from France, French officers and civil servants serving with the Alliance were far less enthusiastic about the change than was their President.

This blending of different nationalities throughout the structure of the NATO organization has been one of its triumphs, as a diplomatic instrument, and one of its weaknesses as an effective political organization. The efficiency necessary for this effectiveness of NATO as an institution, that is, as an organism that is not just the sum of its member states—whether in efficiency of administration, communications or political bargaining—has rarely been given priority over the sensitive question of the distribution of posts and perquisites among the various nations. Thus the nationalities of the various military commanders have always reflected the relative import-ance of the member states, with posts being nicely balanced or rotated among nationalities in order to preserve both a common and individual sense of national dignity.

This anxiety to observe the diplomatic niceties has helped to secure domestic support at many sensitive moments—even from national parliaments: 'burden-sharing' problems, for example, would undoubtedly have been much more difficult to resolve than has been the case had it not been for the sense of common involvement and joint responsibility that has been fostered at working levels of administration. Operating with two official languages, but really one unofficial one, i.e. 'American', the NATO institutions have worked remarkably well and have led to a degree of co-operation—especially in the military field—that would have been unthinkable before the establishment of NATO.

Unfortunately, this structure has not been necessarily one that could be relied upon under stress, or one that would at least be amenable to the subtleties which give real force to bureau-cracies. There has not been, in effect, the same kind of 'life of its own' in the NATO bureaucracy as one might find in a national bureaucracy, with its procedures for making senior appointments from within a career structure and with its jealously-guarded informal prerogatives. The secondment of officers and civilians from outside, and the notion that civilian staff, however 'professional', still remain nationals of different countries, have prevented the NATO bureaucracies—military and civilian—from arrogating to themselves the kind of power that would have made them a true force to be reckoned with in the conclusion of policy. This problem has been, of course, complicated by the isolation of the commands and civilian staffs from individual governments; and at times, the problem has arisen of national delegations to the North Atlantic Council becoming suspect as far as governments in home capitals have been concerned. This is a problem common to diplomatic services everywhere, compounded by the institutional framework of NATO that in itself creates allegiances—but allegiances that lack their own true sovereignty or constituency.

Finally, these difficulties have been increased somewhat by the need to have a common standard for handling classified information—thereby retarding the flow of information within the Alliance, or at least ensuring that matters of gravest importance would be dealt with in contexts where there is less chance of compromise. For the same reasons, there has also been an outward appearance of NATO aims and goals—shared by all —that has necessarily obscured the real complexities of diplomatic relations, and indeed, may have helped statesmen to overlook the importance of the complaints made by countries like France concerning the issue of political influence exercised by various member states within the Alliance.

It may be concluded, therefore, that the institutions of NATO have served the Alliance well in implementing agreed policies. But they have been unable, perhaps inevitably, to affect seriously the complicated processes of diplomatic bargaining that have been the life-blood of the Alliance and the relations conducted among fifteen nations within that context.

As an institution, the Warsaw Treaty Organization has had a radically different history from that of NATO. This would not be apparent from a simple reading of the two treaties, however, which are remarkably similar. Indeed, the Warsaw Treaty of Friendship, Co-operation and Mutual Assistance (Appendix 3) shows a greater concern with general problems of peace and security embracing the entire European Continent than does the North Atlantic Treaty; it provides specifically that a General European Treaty of Collective Security would automatically replace the Warsaw Pact; and it also contains specific references to the 'universal reduction of armaments'. In addition, the Warsaw Pact contains references to co-operative arrangements—not unlike Article Two of the North Atlantic Treaty.

On more concrete matters, it provides that 'in the event of armed attack in Europe on one or more of the Parties to the Treaty' there should immediately be decisions by each of the other Parties 'individually or in agreement' to 'come to the assistance of the state or states attacked with all such means as it deems necessary'. There is certainly little difference to be found here between the two Treaties, except in the version of the Warsaw Pact applying to East Germany, which makes its assistance subject to the determination of the states attacked, and in the provision limiting the scope of the Pact to *Europe*— i.e. excluding Soviet security problems in Asia.

Of course, the strength or weakness of institutions lies in their practice, not in their promise. And the Warsaw Treaty Organization has never become a fully-fledged institution like the one facing it to the West across the division of Europe. This is so despite the fact that the Treaty itself provides specifically for a Political Consultative Committee and a Joint Command— while the North Atlantic Treaty provides only for a Council, which could 'set up such subsidiary bodies as may be necessary'. Yet neither of these Warsaw Pact institutions—nor the Permanent Commission on foreign affairs nor The Joint Secretariat, subsidiary institutions that were agreed to separately— has the significance within the context of Eastern *bloc* security that the North Atlantic Council and Allied Command Europe have had within that of the West.

At least this was clearly the pattern within the Warsaw Pact through the end of the 1950s; indeed, the Political Consultative Committee only met three times during the first five years of the Pact, despite an agreement to meet not less than twice a year; and it was only in October 1961 that the first joint military exercises were held in the East. Furthermore, it was only after the beginning of the 1960s that the Soviet Union began to place any real reliance upon satellite forces, in order to permit reductions in Soviet troops. At first this reliance came during a period of greater Soviet emphasis upon the use of nuclear weapons in any European war, where the limited roles for conventional forces could be played by the satellite states; later the Russians developed even more need for satellite forces as Moscow took tentative steps to downgrade the role of nuclear weapons and to make it possible to fight a European war for a longer time in a non-nuclear phase.

Finally, so far as is known in the West, there has never been a systematic development of institutions within the Warsaw Pact, entailing, as in NATO, the careful allocation of subsidiary commands or of posts in civilian agencies among competing nationalities. Most of the reins are still held in Soviet hands, with staff planning apparently carried out in Moscow, although from time to time military exercises have been held under the nominal command of satellite officers.

This lack of an institutional structure for coalition politics has not saved the Soviet Union from problems of sharing its influence with its satellite allies, however. In fact, the Russians have come to rely increasingly upon the Warsaw Pact as a channel for influence and as a focus for Eastern *bloc* cohesion—a process that has advanced precisely as the 'threat' of attack from the West has been seen to recede, and tendencies towards 'polycentrism' have emerged in the East. As this has happened the Russians have looked more to the Warsaw Pact as a means for linking its satellites more firmly within a context of security where, more even than in economic matters that are covered by the Council for Mutual Economic Assistance (COMECON), there can be seen to be a dependence of Eastern European nations upon Russian leadership and support. COMECON, created in 1949 but only really active after about 1955, has until recent years been the principal mechanism to supplement Soviet bilateral treaties with the satellite states and, through a 'division of labour', has sought to bind them more closely to the Soviet Union. However, this has apparently not met Russian demands for 'security' in an age of *détente* and increasing East-West economic ties. Partly as a result of this process, there have begun to develop within the Warsaw Pact some of the same problems that have plagued NATO over a much longer period of time.

Beginning in the middle 1960s, there began to be a series of limited challenges to Russian dominance within the Warsaw Pact—led by Roumania, from about 1965 onwards—as the institutions of the Alliance began to take on more importance for all the nations concerned. In part, this reflected an ambivalence on the part of various East European regimes about the use of Soviet power to put down revolts such as the one in Hungary—a revolt that may be seen as one reason for the Russians' placing an increasing value on the role of the Warsaw Pact in the following years, and for their concluding a number of 'status of forces' agreements with satellite states. In 1968, for example, pressure from other Eastern European regimes certainly contributed to the Russian decision to intervene in Czechoslovakia, lest the Czech 'infection' of liberalism spread elsewhere; but at the same time the co-operation of four Warsaw Pact countries in the actual invasion was undoubtedly designed in Moscow to add legitimacy to Soviet actions, and to play down the purely Soviet character of the political decision and military operations. And the use of a Warsaw Pact context may also reflect Russian anxiety lest the invasion be seen in the West as solely a Soviet venture that could have direct implications for Soviet-American *détente*.

But while four Warsaw Pact nations—East Germany, Poland, Hungary, Bulgaria—co-operated in the invasion of Czechoslovakia, there has at times still been an ambivalent attitude, even among these regimes, about the circumstances in which Soviet power would be used for purposes inside the Pact instead of being reserved for use against an attack from the West. And, the further away an Eastern *bloc* state is located geographically from the potential 'front line' of hostilities—that is on the direct axis between West Germany and the Soviet Union—the less there has been enthusiasm for tight institutional arrangements within the Pact itself. Indeed, over the years there has developed a dichotomy within the Warsaw Pact, between the so-called 'Northern Tier' nations of East Germany, Poland and Czechoslovakia—nations which were more politically vulnerable to real or stimulated fears of West German revanchism—and those states further to the east: Bulgaria, Roumania, and Albania. These latter three nations have each challenged the Soviet Union in one way or another: Bulgaria through a reputed 'plot' in 1965; Roumania by a consistent search for greater national independence; and Albania by effectively withdrawing from the Pact in March 1961, and formally doing so in late 1968.

The ambivalence felt in several East European countries about the role of Warsaw Pact institutions and the possible uses of Soviet power can be seen in the contrast between Czechoslovakia and Roumania. The former, during its phase of liberalization in 1968, was constrained to reassure the Soviet Union about its loyalty to the Warsaw Pact—thereby hoping to avoid the mistake made by the Hungarian regime of Imre Nagy in denouncing the Pact during the 1956 revolution. But at the same time the Dubček regime in Prague was reluctant to take an active part in Warsaw Pact exercises that would only provide an excuse for the stationing of Russian troops on Czech soil.

Unfortunately, the Czechs could not reconcile this dilemma within a framework of East European security; indeed, it was Soviet communications units left behind in Czechoslovakia, and Warsaw Pact forces ostensibly on regular manoeuvres near its borders, that facilitated the joint invasion in August 1968.

For the Roumanians, on the other hand, an ambivalence about institutions has usually led them to challenge, rather than to accept, Soviet views. Lying geographically outside the path of a potential attack from the West, the Roumanians have felt better able to resist Soviet efforts to strengthen the institutional structure of the Warsaw Pact. Over the past five years or so, it has been the regime in Bucharest that has brought to light the growing complexities surrounding the development of Pact institutions, and the growing resentment in Eastern Europe about Russian domination of them. For example, the Roumanians have challenged the practice whereby Warsaw Pact forces are always commanded by a Soviet general.

This is a somewhat different matter from the practice of always allocating the job of Supreme Allied Commander, Europe, to an American general. Within the Warsaw Pact, for example, there is hardly more than a pretence of an integrated command structure with important subordinate posts that could be allocated among the East European allies. Furthermore, there is an even greater reliance in the East on the role of Soviet forces, particularly the role closely connected with the use of nuclear weapons: after all, the Russians have never tried to make the fine distinctions between nuclear and 'conventional' war that have been made by the Americans. And the Russians have not felt constrained to go even as far as the Americans in providing their Allies with nuclear weapons, even under the so-called 'two-key' system, where agreement of both donor and recipient nation is required for their use. In the Warsaw Pact, the Russians have, in recent years, provided short-range missiles to some of their Eastern *bloc* Allies, but there is no evidence that the nuclear warheads for these missiles have been provided to the Allies or that they are even stockpiled outside the Soviet Union.

This last development seems to reflect the existence of a problem somewhat similar to that found within NATO; but there has certainly not been a full-scale 'nuclear sharing' problem in the Warsaw Pact like that seen in the West, at least in part because of the Russians' reliance in their strategic doctrine upon the use of nuclear weapons at an early stage of conflict. But this is a matter that will bear close attention in the next few years.

In recent years, however, there has been a growing effort by the Soviet Union to provide something like an integrated command structure for the Warsaw Pact. But the relationship between this effort and the provision of increased fighting ability on the part of satellite forces is not clearly established. It is likely that the Soviet Union, having turned to its security pact as a more reliable instrument than its economic treaty, COMECON, in channelling influence to Eastern Europe, has become more concerned that individual states within the Warsaw Pact should be seen to play a co-operative alliance role. Such a development would, in theory, also provide a context for more effective co-operation *among* the East European allies, particularly in providing a form of 'cohesion' or 'discipline' within a Soviet concept of security needs.

The Roumanians have consistently opposed this Soviet effort over the years, especially in cases where it has been obvious that the new arrangements would merely work to the Russians' political advantage within the Alliance. Where there has seemed a chance that closer co-operation would give satellite governments—meaning Roumania—more influence on Soviet policy and, particularly, on the conditions under which Russian forces would have the right to be stationed or manoeuvre on satellite territory, then the Roumanians have appeared to be more receptive. In any event, following the invasion of Czechoslovakia, the Roumanians modified their lonely stand within the Warsaw Pact, apparently to test the limits of Soviet patience before continuing their effort to define the division of influence within the alliance. Yet by early 1969 the Roumanians were again attempting to broaden the scope for national action within the context of the Warsaw Pact, although they were a bit more cautious than before in judging the limits placed by the Russians on their definition of security in Europe. In March 1969, the Warsaw Pact Powers 'endorsed' a 'Statute on the Committee of Defence Ministers'; adopted a new statute on 'Joint Armed Forces and the Integrated Command'; and adopted 'other documents designed to bring about a further improvement in the structure and organs of administration of the defence organization of the Treaty'. But what these cryptic announcements would mean in practical terms was not immediately apparent.

This process of defining relative influence within the institutions of the Warsaw Pact—and in the formal and informal consultative councils—also involved the problem known in NATO as burden-sharing. Little is known of the actual division of the costs of alliance among nations within the Warsaw Pact, but a Roumanian diplomatic manoeuvre in May 1966, reflecting its opposition to 'foreign bases', did indicate that the allied states had been expected to contribute to the financing of Soviet forces stationed in Eastern Europe. To this Roumania was opposed, as a function of the unsettled questions of sovereignty within the Pact and the amount of relative 'influence' gained by the Soviet Union by having forces on the territory of its satellites. Like the question of a more closely integrated command structure, this question also does not seem to have yet been resolved satisfactorily by the Warsaw Pact states, although certainly the Roumanians have lost their bid to have the command of Warsaw Pact forces rotate among the member states. The Russians, clearly, are not yet ready to pay such a high price for an increase in an alliance 'cohesion' that may itself depend largely upon the possibilities of independent Soviet military action within the context of the Warsaw Pact. This is a factor that is very important, for example, in the selection of sites for joint manoeuvres, as was demonstrated by the invasion of Czechoslovakia, and which has now been extended and 'codified' by the Brezhnev Doctrine on the limited sovereignty of states in the so-called Socialist Commonwealth, thereby overcoming a structural weakness—from the Russian point of view—in the Warsaw Pact itself.

In any event, the Russians' greater reliance upon Warsaw Pact forces in European security—a development which was designed, in part, to help justify the reduction of Soviet conventional forces at the beginning of the decade—has led to a greater elaboration of the Pact's institutional structure, even though the network of bilateral treaties woven by the Russians in the 1940s has mostly been renewed and revised, beginning with Czechoslovakia in 1963, East Germany in 1964 (a new treaty), and Poland in 1965; and these bilateral treaties retain their fundamental importance to Moscow, and, in some cases, entail more binding commitments of mutual alliance than does the Warsaw Pact itself. Yet this process of elaboration, in turn,

61

has gone together with a modernization of Warsaw Pact forces and the development of a greater combat role for them, as opposed to their previous role as a sort of forward air defence for the Soviet Union. These developments, of course, could potentially increase Russian anxieties about the loyalty of individual satellite armies—for example, Czechoslovakia's well-equipped army of more than fourteen divisions—during a period of internal unrest within the Eastern *bloc*. Here, there lies some support for the view that the Soviet invasion of Czechoslovakia derived in part from genuine concerns in Moscow about security: that is, with the development of more effective Warsaw Pact forces, the Russians may feel a greater need to be assured of the loyalty of individual states and of the strength of interstate cohesion for purposes of discipline within the Pact— again, as the Pact was used to provide the context within which to mount the invasion of Czechoslovakia.

This role to be played by satellite forces in helping to maintain an internal discipline within the Pact has become all the more important for the Soviet Union, using its extremely broad definition of its own 'security' in an era of *détente* with the United States: that is, there is now a common interest in making sure that the NATO Powers can distinguish between the movement of additional Soviet troops into Eastern Europe for internal uses, as opposed to preparations for attack against the West. And the danger of misperception by the West, which could lead to a mutual process of troop reinforcements and the risk of accidental war, has placed a premium on the Russians' not moving additional forces into Eastern Europe—at least not without the most careful assurances to the NATO nations. These assurances were given in August 1968; and they were accepted by NATO although, as will be discussed in Chapter 6, this process in itself had a disruptive effect on the possibilities for East-West *détente*. Therefore, for the Russians, Eastern *bloc* forces could relieve the Russians of the need to risk a crisis with the West by making conventional reinforcements in Eastern Europe; and, of course, the presence of satellite forces rather than Russian reinforcements would also inhibit escalation of any crisis with the West, and would be a useful buffer at the outbreak of a European war.

In conclusion, the institutional structure and significance of the Warsaw Pact can be seen as a continuous process of evolution, extending from the earliest days of the Pact in which institutions existed only on paper, and in which the Pact was more a propaganda counter to West Germany's entering NATO than anything else, to a time when some real problems— of cohesion, of command structure, of burden-sharing—have emerged as a function of the greater elaboration of the Pact and reliance of the Soviet Union on it for security, both against any 'threat' from the West, and against erosion of the Russian position of influence within the Eastern *bloc* itself. But for all the similarities of this process with problems evident in NATO's institutions, major differences caution one against seeing NATO and the Warsaw Pact as complementary institutions, except in the most fundamental terms of the super-power guarantees to the military security of the Continent, and the symbiotic relationship imposed upon alliances in confrontation. The Warsaw Pact has never become a particularly effective forum for channelling influence back *to* the super-power, although the Roumanians have succeeded from time to time in thwarting Russia's plans for strengthening the Pact as a vehicle for its own influence in Eastern Europe. Furthermore, the Pact has not been as successful as NATO in the West in co-ordinating the military effort of the Eastern *bloc* states, and it certainly has never become the focus for grander efforts by the Eastern European states, themselves, to proceed to more elaborate forms of functional integration. Indeed, in the late 1940s, the Russians blocked movements towards integration among the Balkan states, in order to preserve unimpaired their own bilateral lines of influence. Insofar as roles of co-ordination and integration have been played at all by institutions in the East, they have taken place more within the context of COMECON.

Even more important, however, in distinguishing NATO from the Warsaw Pact as an institution has been the sense of assurance throughout the NATO Alliance concerning its basic political purposes and the concern of the United States for the political and economic growth of Western Europe. In the Warsaw Pact, on the other hand, there has been no such sense of assurance, since it has rarely been clear whether or in what manner the Soviet Union would accommodate itself to the needs and interests of its East European Allies. This difference between the two Alliances is partly reflected in the process of their creation: NATO was largely a European creation that co-opted the United States; the Warsaw Pact was essentially a function of Soviet foreign policy from the beginning. As a result, comparisons of the *political* purposes of the two Alliances must be made very carefully indeed, and with a host of qualifications borne in mind.

Finally, there are certain facts of geography that have prevented there being a symmetry of relationship between the Americans and NATO, on the one hand, and the Russians and the Warsaw Pact on the other. The most important of these facts, of course, is the close proximity of the Soviet Union to all its Eastern Allies, and the overshadowing of Eastern Europe by Soviet military power, of whatever form—a fact that certainly helps to reduce the chances of a crisis of confidence in the Warsaw Pact (a problem of 'credibility') concerning Soviet military involvement in East Europe's defence. But certainly over the last few years, the importance of the Warsaw Pact as an institution in the development of European security has become more important, first as a focus of super-power influence; second as an element of stability for the whole Continent; and third as a source of problems among the Pact allies. As such, it deserves to be given even more attention in the future in any study of the problems of European security.

Chapter 4

Strategy

Histories of NATO are usually written in terms of the strategic problems that faced the Allies, and of the steps they took—successfully or not—to solve them. This study cannot ignore these problems, as some comprehension of strategic matters is essential to understanding the history of NATO. Above all, understanding strategic problems is important for their impact upon politics, and the ways in which they have helped shape political relations, not only within the Alliance, but also as between East and West.

The strategic doctrine of NATO began, as noted in an earlier chapter, with the so-called 'forward strategy', a political doctrine designed to protect the nations of Western Europe against a putative threat as far forward geographically in Central Europe as possible: that is, in West Germany itself. And, as discussed before, the adoption of this doctrine meant that German forces would have to be involved if it were to be at all viable.

It took many years to implement the forward strategy; indeed, it was not until the 1960s that the conventional component of the strategy came to be realized. Throughout the early years, there were repeated efforts, primarily by the United States, to stimulate the Allies to meet the ideal force levels agreed at the Lisbon meeting of the North Atlantic Council in February 1952—i.e. 25 to 30 divisions on the Central Front as opposed to the 15 there were at the time. But for a variety of reasons, achieving these goals continued to elude the military planners. Of course, there was still no real consensus within the Alliance about the practical nature and extent of the Soviet threat, though there was a general sort of agreement in theory. These failures to meet force quotas were good indications of the true feelings of member countries about how seriously they were taking their parlous state.

Of course, from the beginning of the Alliance not all the NATO nations were actually involved in providing forces, and as time went on, many of them never really became deeply involved in this effort. Portugal, for example, has never contributed troops to Allied Command Europe; Iceland has had no forces at all (and has, therefore, been represented on the Military Committee of the Alliance by a civilian). And, throughout the years, Norway has never allowed Allied troops to be stationed permanently on her soil, except for short periods of time for the purpose of training exercises. Finally, neither Norway nor Denmark has allowed nuclear weapons to be based on her territory.

These are illuminating facts, in view of the tremendous uproar—particularly in the United States—when France withdrew from Allied Command Europe in 1966, as the final act in a three-stage withdrawal from the Allied military commands—the first two stages entailing withdrawal of the French fleets from their 'earmarked' status in the commands covering the Atlantic Ocean and Mediterranean Sea, respectively. French forces and territory, of course, constituted an important part of the defence structure of the vital Central Front, and there was at least a marginal case for believing that French force withdrawals from Allied Command Europe would affect NATO strategy.

But in reality, these withdrawals—as well as those planned by Canada in 1969—had their most significant effect in *appearing* to affect NATO strategy, or, at least, to affect the sense of common purpose, or cohesion, upon which planners had long based the credibility of the conventional component of the NATO deterrent. It had been this way throughout the history of NATO—i.e. the appearance of a viable strategy often came to stand for reality, not so much in Russian eyes (and we do not yet know what the Russians thought of NATO's changes in strategy over the years) as in the eyes of NATO beholders themselves. Indeed, the continuing gap between NATO's actual strategic posture on the ground—which did contribute to Soviet inactivity all those years—and the 'ideal' laid down as the basis for inter-Allied bargaining about the sharing of common burdens, helped to focus attention on the half-empty bottle, not the half-full one. In effect, there was no real frame of reference that encompassed both the strategic posture of NATO and what was going on in terms of 'threat' on the other side of confrontation in Europe, at least not a frame of reference that could be translated into Alliance politics, let alone break the continuing context of military confrontation that was imposing a logic of its own. Like the institutions of NATO, its strategy acquired a personality that had to be fulfilled, almost without reference to the causes that had brought it into being in the first place.

As the 1950s wore on, so did the debates about NATO's strategic posture. 1954–55, the 'Year of Maximum Danger', came and went, without anyone's saying that the danger had then diminished. The goals were not fulfilled. But, of course, NATO's strategy was not based entirely on ground troops and fighter aircraft. Since at least 1948, the United States had been providing a form of nuclear deterrent for Europe, first with B-29s ostentatiously based in England during the Berlin blockade—although it now seems clear that these bombers did not actually carry nuclear weapons at first and were more of symbolic significance than of anything else. Later, this deterrent was centred on a great complex of bomber bases strung out around the world. Therefore, from the first, the American nuclear arsenal was implicitly a part of NATO strategy. If there had been a major Russian attack on Western Europe, America would have been expected at some point to unleash its bombers. After all, the United States was until the late 1950s practically invulnerable to Russian nuclear attack, and could make this pledge to her Allies with relative impunity.

As the decade progressed, Europeans put increasing reliance

on this American nuclear guarantee, partly from economic motives, since this guarantee would, in theory, relieve them of the need to provide all the conventional forces which the ideal strategy of conventional defence—and the force goals adopted at Lisbon—demanded. But European behaviour stemmed only partly from economic motives. It soon became obvious that no Western European country that might be a battlefield in the Third World War had much to look forward to in a conventional defence; the destruction would be catastrophic, even if the Allies eventually prevailed. This argument applied with strongest force to West Germany, which had been a major battlefield of the Second World War, and promised to be one in the Third, and this attitude helps to explain some of the special problems that arose in the Alliance when the West Germans were admitted; indeed they, with the Americans, were always willing to take most seriously the consequences of underestimating the Russians' ability or willingness to attack the NATO nations.

This chain of reasoning meant that there was considerable appeal in Western Europe for a policy of *deterring* Russian attack, even if the response to this attack were largely confined in practice to nuclear weapons. And, of course, the chief means for accomplishing this strategy, whether of deterrence or of 'defence' following the failure of deterrence, was through use of the American nuclear arsenal.

Between January 1954 and December 1956, the Allies debated whether NATO military planning should be based on the making available of relatively small nuclear weapons not then based in Europe—weapons called, by what has often seemed to be an unfortunate misnomer, 'tactical'—for use against enemy forces and communications. This debate took place although no one has ever adequately explained how it would be possible in densely populated Europe to use a weapon roughly of the size of those used at Hiroshima and Nagasaki and yet talk of 'tactical' instead of 'strategic' destruction. This point has not been lost on many Europeans over the years.

In any event, at the end of the debate—which was long, boring and esoteric—the North Atlantic Council at the end of 1956 formally adopted a new strategy which really did little more than formalize existing attitudes, and accept, finally, the concept implicit in a Council decision of December 1954 to plan on the basis that nuclear weapons would be available, whether or not the enemy used them first. According to this concept, the Allies would only mount a conventional defence of Western Europe for a very short time, and then would rely upon the United States to introduce nuclear weapons, presumably leading up to a major nuclear war. The only reason for having conventional weapons at all was to serve as a 'trip-wire' or 'plate glass window' that would signal the start of the tactical phase of the nuclear war.

This seemed to many to be a sound strategy—particularly since this was still the period of the American 'massive retaliation' doctrine, and much emphasis was placed on the potency and viability of the American nuclear arsenal, particularly since the United States appeared to remain effectively invulnerable to direct Soviet attack.

But in political terms, the adoption of the new NATO strategy marked the beginning of an era in which the relationship of the United States to its Allies in Europe came increasingly to be debated in terms of nuclear strategy. And if there had been any prospect of any real division of military labour as between the United States and her Allies—a division of labour which could have had meaning in terms of the sharing of political influence—then that time was now passing. The Europeans now accepted that only the United States could provide the necessary defence of the Continent, not just in terms of the psychological support that an American guarantee would provide, but also in hard practical terms as well. It was not entirely a coincidence that this period also marked the beginning of a process in which the Allies began thinking seriously about means of broadening the scope of the Alliance, in order to build upon the common military effort. If the

Europeans were to be even more dependent upon the Americans than before, then there might at least be some means for spreading the influence available within the Alliance in other fields, including the so-called non-military uses of NÁTO, to be described at length in Chapter 5.

But before long this NATO strategy was under review. Significantly, the review began in Europe at the end of 1956, under the sponsorship of the new Supreme Allied Commander, Europe, General Lauris Norstad. In 1957 the Military Committee of NATO adopted a major study that, although it was designed to implement decisions concerning the use of tactical nuclear weapons, actually outlined a new form of strategic and political relationship between conventional and nuclear arms. Implicit in the proposals made in this study—the so-called 'MC-70'—there should no longer be merely a plate glass window, or trip-wire, but rather sufficient conventional forces (a shield), not for the purpose of fighting a truly conventional war (with all the destruction that this implied for the 'forward' countries), but rather in order to force the enemy to 'pause' after the initial stages of an attack in order to re-calculate the balance of risks and advantages, before continuing the attack and before forcing the US to unleash its nuclear arsenal. This was, indeed, the beginning of an era in which the Russians were no longer to be regarded within NATO as infallible giants whose first probing attack could reasonably be taken as a necessarily successful all-out drive to the English Channel. What would happen, the European allies were beginning to ask, if the Soviets did not believe that the US would use nuclear weapons—that is, would start a world-wide nuclear war—just for the defence of a small corner of NATO territory? Surely, the reasoning went, the Russians should be given an opportunity to think again, after the beginning of a conventional attack, before the world was blown up?

This doctrine seemed to make eminent sense, although it had the unfortunate implication of requiring more conventional forces than had been planned under the trip-wire doctrine, and of requiring more pressure on the European Allies to build up the levels of their conventional forces. But at least with a 'pause' doctrine more sanity would be introduced into NATO strategy and the awful prospect of a nuclear war would not be seen as something that happened by accident, or as the outgrowth of a merely logical process. There would be the possibility of intermediate responses and second thoughts.

With this report of the Military Committee, urging a revised strategy, the first glimmerings of an attitude of *détente* in the West began to appear—an attitude that could comprehend the probable nature of conflict in Europe as it would actually transpire, and that could accept the need to find a way out of the terrible nuclear dilemmas that had been created by the cataclysmic doctrines evolved when there was seen—especially by the Americans—to be an implacable Soviet military threat to Western Europe.

The development of a 'pause' doctrine and its interaction with the role envisaged for the American nuclear deterrent then entered a phase that witnessed perhaps the most subtle political and strategic interchanges in the history of the Alliance. These interchanges demonstrated time after time the dependence of the Europeans on the Americans, and repeatedly strained relations across the Atlantic. That is not to say that perceptions of the problem were accurate—that either a strategic response based on 'pause' or one based on early first use of nuclear weapons was the only one to deter the particular Soviet threat. After all, there was still little attempt to relate NATO strategy to a conception of Soviet threat that was unclouded by the context of conflict that had solidified at the beginning of the 1950s.

In any case, the most important event in changing the American and European relationship in terms of politics and strategy occurred in the period 1956–58: when the United States rapidly lost the protection of being impervious to Soviet nuclear attack. A Soviet bomber attack on the US had been possible for a short time, but suddenly, after the launching of

Sputnik in October 1957, America began to appear genuinely vulnerable. This was not something that worried only the Europeans, of course. The Americans themselves began to think seriously about the structure of their nuclear deterrent power (with the civilians finally taking over from the military thinkers on the subject), and began to worry about constructing a system of deterrence that could survive any Soviet attack and remain viable. In practice, this meant building invulnerable missiles underground (*Minuteman*) and under water (*Polaris*).

In Europe, however, a new crisis was brewing. Since the United States was now seen to be directly vulnerable to Soviet attack, how could one believe that the Americans would risk their own destruction in order to preserve the security from Soviet attack of America's European Allies? This was a line of reasoning pursued by the Gaullists with increasing persistence over the years. Thus was ushered in a long period of fundamental uncertainty and a complex political process within the Alliance which became known as the 'nuclear sharing' problem.

There have always been at least two elements to this problem: first, how could the United States convince the Russians that threats of nuclear retaliation against Russian conventional attack in Europe were credible—i.e. that Europe was of such political worth to the United States that any risk would be justified? Second, how could the Americans convince their Allies of the same thing? Throughout the years in which this issue has been important it has proved far easier to accomplish the first of these tasks than the second—for perhaps a simple reason: the Russians had only to calculate the risks of *gaining* political objectives—while the West Europeans were concerned about *losing* political values, as well as defining a fundamental political relationship to the United States.

It has been perhaps one of the greatest political miracles of the twentieth century that America's Allies in Europe have continued to believe her commitments to defend them with nuclear weapons for as long as they have. In 1966, for example, General de Gaulle put together a very logical case for withdrawing his forces from Allied Command Europe. The risks of being drawn into a nuclear war because of some American misadventure elsewhere had gone up, he argued; and the credibility of the American nuclear guarantee had gone down as the Americans had become increasingly vulnerable to Russian nuclear attack. Such was his case; and in many respects it was a compelling one. But few Europeans have ever agreed with him. And that fact speaks, perhaps, of an American diplomatic triumph achieved through a period that includes perhaps the most incredible series of American diplomatic blunders in the history of the North Atlantic Treaty Organization.

To understand this process, one must examine more closely a major event in the development of NATO strategy: a highly controversial speech made by the then American Secretary of Defense, Mr Robert McNamara, to the North Atlantic Council in May of 1962. The speech itself has never been made public, but what was reputed to be a reasonable facsimile of it was contained in a speech delivered at Ann Arbor, Michigan, that summer. What did Mr McNamara say that aroused such consternation among America's European Allies? And why had he chosen to put the cat among the pigeons at this particular moment?

The answers to these questions can best be explained indirectly within the context of the intricacies of nuclear strategy, and that unpredictable quantity known as the diplomatic confidence of one nation in another. Quite simply, in 1962 the United States was facing some hard choices with regard to her own relations with the Soviet Union—relations that contained elements of the more abstruse strategic doctrines—and with regard to her relations with the European members of NATO. Almost imperceptibly, some of the basic interests of the US and European members of the Alliance were drifting apart.

Mr McNamara's speech also came at a time when there was increasing concern in the United States about other nuclear deterrent forces owned by NATO Allies. There were at that time two of them in the works, one British—already in being—

and one French that was being developed. Neither of them seemed to be particularly relevant, strategically, when compared with the overwhelming strategic might of the Americans and Russians. Indeed, both the British and French deterrents were planned before the formal elaboration of the so-called doctrine of 'proportional deterrence'—i.e. the idea, in this instance, that nothing that the Russians could gain from the destruction of, say, Britain could possibly be worth the loss of those few Russian cities that the British V-Bomber force (now her *Polaris* missiles) could always be sure of destroying.

But the existence of the British force, and the development of the French one—then largely conceived as part of the coin of great-power status—did pose some real problems for the United States. Basically, the Americans were becoming increasingly concerned about the problems of controlling a nuclear war if one should, for any reason, begin—concern that was a logical extension of the thinking surrounding the 'pause' doctrine itself. How could a nuclear war be brought effectively under control? How could destruction be limited? How, indeed, could a nuclear war be conducted, so as not to become just one long spasm of nuclear explosions from its beginning to the end of the world?

The answers to these questions were slowly evolved in the American Defense Department, in one of the more abstruse elaborations of doctrine that have marked the development of the whole depressing—and arguably insane—subject of nuclear strategy. There should be, according to the theory, an attempt to spare the enemy's cities—in this case Russian cities—in the first nuclear exchange of a nuclear war, in order to give leaders in the Kremlin an incentive not to strike American cities. Ideally, the battle would be fought out by firing nuclear missiles against nuclear missiles, with a chance, therefore, that the madness that would characterize any nuclear war could be brought to a halt.

Unfortunately, there was a basic flaw in this proposition: at that time the US possessed such a superiority of nuclear weapons that the Soviet Union could never survive a contest in which America destroyed all of Russia's missiles and bombers, yet had some of her own left over to hold Russian cities hostage. And, indeed, the Russians never agreed to play the game as it was conceived in the Pentagon. But it seemed an attractive idea to the Americans at the time, and this so-called 'no cities' (or 'counterforce') doctrine gained in appeal.

But here the European independent deterrents posed a problem as well as an incentive to further nuclear proliferation. They could, for a start, complicate the problem of controlling a nuclear war—that is, in order to bring a nuclear war to a halt, central direction of diplomatic interchanges was required as well as firm limits on the possible use of *all* nuclear weapons on each side of the possible nuclear confrontation. The Russians, of course, had never relaxed their grip on the satellite nations of Eastern Europe to the point that any of them could consider acquiring nuclear weapons, so Moscow did not have to face this problem.

But the Americans had not exercised such firm control of their Allies. In addition, there was a possibility that use of the European deterrent forces could actually start a nuclear war on its own—a so-called 'catalytic war'—thereby involving the Americans in a nuclear war with the Soviet Union whether either super-power wanted one or not. The Americans themselves also thought that the Russians would be concerned that one of these smaller nuclear arsenals could go off by accident or miscalculation, and would therefore be more jittery; but for the Europeans, there was seen to be a certain value—a certain confidence—in having the ability to involve the US in a nuclear war on behalf of Europe even if the US President proved reluctant in the event. After all, were not the US troops in Germany really only serving as hostages to the Europeans in order to demonstrate the US nuclear commitment? Therefore, American efforts to minimize the importance of nuclear weapons and discourage their production led to the raising of a number of eyebrows on the Continent.

This was the context within which one must view Mr McNamara's speech—the enunciation of the famous 'McNamara Doctrine'—which reviewed some of the less controversial aspects of this discussion. Most importantly, he downgraded the special nature of nuclear weapons, and argued that they should be used primarily for attacks on enemy forces, not on enemy cities, at least in the first instance after a nuclear war had begun.

As discussed above, the Europeans were already uneasy about the credibility of the US deterrent. But there was even more to the McNamara speech to concern the Europeans: the US Defense Secretary also minimized the importance of European deterrents, and stressed the need for central control. In passing he tried to reassure the Allies about American nuclear guarantees to Europe; but at the same time he argued that deterrence of Soviet attack in Europe would actually be enhanced by having more conventional forces on the ground— something vaguely termed 'flexible response'—and then—as the most cardinal sin—went beyond that to declare that a conventional defence of Western Europe was even becoming possible.

Pandemonium broke loose in Europe—largely among people who had no understanding of the complexities of nuclear problems (a category which has always included almost everyone), as well as among people who did. But this reaction stemmed not so much from the content of the McNamara Doctrine as it was enunciated, as it did from the psychological overtones of the whole process. Here, suddenly, the United States seemed to be backing away from the unequivocal nature of its commitment to NATO—a commitment that had remained credible despite the fact that the United States was growing directly vulnerable to Russian nuclear attack. It was true, of course, that the new doctrine might actually have made these guarantees more credible to the Russians by the strict logic of deterrence—that is, by not threatening the end of the world over the loss of a small parcel of Western European territory. But the two facets, the problem of preserving credibility with the Russians on the one hand and the European Allies on the other, came into direct conflict. As usual, it was the need to reassure the Allies that caused the Americans the greater headaches.

It was almost entirely a psychological problem. The American nuclear guarantee had rested upon a promise—and blind faith on the part of Europeans. America, once Fortress America, had renounced her isolation in order to participate in the defence of Europe. This commitment therefore had to be complete, whole, and not subject to a moment's doubt. But suddenly the illusion of certainty was being shattered; whatever the intentions of the American government or the merits of the strategic arguments, the purity of the American commitment was compromised. And no one was more surprised to learn of this than the Americans themselves, who had believed they were meeting a straightforward and logical problem with a straightforward and logical solution.

The capstone to all this concern was the emphasis Mr McNamara had placed upon European conventional arms. This was already a shibboleth—or, better, a sort of standing joke—in which the Americans asked and never succeeded in getting the Europeans to match the agreed force goals. But at the beginning of the 1960s, as suggested above, it was seen in Europe actually to be dangerous to have too many conventional forces in being. This was so not just because such a situation might turn a country like Germany into a devastated battleground before the American President took his decision to use nuclear weapons, but that he might not take that decision at all. This fear, of course, was based on a logical deduction that was really nonsense in view of the obvious—if irrational—willingness of successive American governments and the American people to risk all on Europe's behalf.

But now, with the McNamara speech, the problem was firmly thrust upon the Alliance. And Mr McNamara had made the problem about as bad as he could possibly have done by appearing to talk about an actual conventional defence of the

Continent. No matter that this might actually now be within the realm of possibility, given the almost unnoticed build-up of NATO forces over the years; no matter that the Soviet 'threat' was being radically reduced from the mythical 175 divisions of 1950 for conventional defence purposes. The impact of the McNamara speech derived from the new doubts sown about the commitment—the fundamental psychological commitment —of the United States. And the problem was suddenly much worse than the remedy Mr McNamara was prescribing for the potential 'nuclear sharing' problem. Therefore, within a short period of time, the whole set of new propositions was quietly put aside, until 1967, when—in a time of *détente*—the 'flexible response' doctrine was formally adopted under another name by NATO's Defence Planning Committee with little fuss or bother. But even this was a modified version of the McNamara strategy; under it NATO would respond to an attack at an appropriate level: but there was no question that flexible response ruled out the use of tactical or strategic nuclear weapons.

The content of the McNamara speech was not the only problem that the Europeans felt in 1962. They also saw it in the context of an apparent insensitivity of the US Government to West European attitudes, an insensitivity particularly evident since the Kennedy Administration had been in-augurated and General Lemnitzer had been sent as a mouth-piece of American policy to replace General Norstad, the man who had been more 'European' than American. During this period, there was a whole series of incidents that might earlier have passed off with relatively little notice, but which now seemed to dramatize the strains of confidence that were growing in the Alliance, and the potentially divergent interests separat-ing the two halves of the Alliance as the context of conflict was working itself out and new issues were arising with regard to securing a stable peace throughout Europe.

In the autumn of 1962, for example, there was what came to be known as the '*Skybolt* incident': the United States rather unceremoniously—as the British tell it—informed London that the *Skybolt* missile, which was being built by the Americans to serve a dual purpose as the next generation of the British deterrent, would have to be cancelled. The Americans cited rapidly rising costs, and the lack of successful flight tests of this ballistic missile that was designed to be launched from strategic bombers. From the point of view of the Americans, this decision to cancel *Skybolt* was a logical one: they no longer needed the missile for their own arsenal, and were therefore abandoning it. But there was obviously little or no consideration for the feelings of the British Government, which still wished to maintain a viable nuclear arsenal—an 'independent deterrent'—if only, as the phrase went, to get Britain a seat at the 'top table' in diplomatic negotiations. There was a simple failure of diplomatic communications somewhere which was quickly seen as symptomatic of the Kennedy Administration's attitude towards Alliance consultations and co-operation.

To make matters worse, there was a hastily called diplomatic gathering between President Kennedy and the British Prime Minister at Nassau, at the end of which—for reasons that remain obscure—the British were offered missiles and related equipment which would enable Britain to build and maintain *Polaris*-type submarines. Thus the British 'independent' deterrent was to be preserved yet a while longer.

However, apparently no one had thought of the repercussions that this decision would have within the rest of the Alliance, particularly on those countries which were growing more sensitive about the problem of America's seeming divergence from the rest of the Alliance on matters of nuclear policy and of dealing diplomatically with the Russians. France, in particular, had some reason for annoyance, and President de Gaulle made a point of ignoring a similar offer of *Polaris* missiles without the warheads that the British were then capable of building for themselves—an offer made to him after the Nassau Conference. He had not been consulted; clearly this was unacceptable. And, if one thinks of this problem in terms of Alliance politics, he was right. Whether he really felt that way or not, he used this incident as one reason for excluding Britain from the Common Market in January 1963 on the grounds that the British were too closely tied in with the Americans to be 'good Europeans': a good ironic touch.

But the most important evidence of the strains developing within the Alliance was provided in October 1962 during the Cuban Missile Crisis. Here was a real testing ground for the viability of Alliance consultations and the sharing of influence. In time of peril—when the safety of the world seemed to be at stake—would the Alliance serve as a focus for reaching vital decisions, or would the United States act in the name of all, with potentially the same consequences (including nuclear war) for all?

The United States chose the latter course. This was not unreasonable, considering the gravity of the situation, and the narrow margin by which disaster was—or at least seemed to have been—averted. Indeed, one would have expected little complaint from the Europeans. Yet this incident fell within the ambit of the growing problem centred on the conflict between America's relations with the Russians, and America's relations with her European Allies. Would the United States ever take her Allies completely into her confidence? Would there ever be any form of common decision on these matters of life and death? And, even more importantly, might the Americans some day deal behind the backs of the Europeans in order to further the cause of American-Soviet understanding at the expense of European interests? These were serious questions that were made worse by President Kennedy's making it very pointedly clear that he had *not* consulted his Allies. Indeed, this problem has only grown in magnitude, and was the chief motive for President Nixon's rather hasty—if hardly eventful—visit to Western Europe at the very beginning of his Administration: namely, to reassure the West Europeans that essential US negotiations with the Russians on vital matters of arms control, which would affect the future security of all concerned, would not be conducted at the expense either of West European interests or of NATO Alliance co-operation. And this growing problem has been the basis for a number of projects designed to demonstrate what is usually called 'crisis management' within the Alliance but which, except for the rather special circumstances surrounding the Berlin crisis of 1958–61, and the establishment of a 'Nuclear Planning Group', has never proved a particularly practical proposition.

At the time of the Cuban Missile Crisis in October 1962, Dean Acheson, the former Secretary of State, was sent to Europe to explain the situation. In a famous confrontation with General de Gaulle, Acheson was asked whether he was seeking French advice or merely informing about US plans. 'Informing' was the honest reply. 'Good,' the general is reputed to have answered, 'I believe in independent decisions.' And from that moment, perhaps, one can date the full awareness in de Gaulle's policy of the need for France to be able to make its *own* independent decisions, if the Americans' prerogative of doing so could obviously compromise the interests of Europe in general and of France in particular.

Thus, formally, began a period in which American governments searched for some way out of the central dilemma of reconciling US-Soviet interests with US-West European relations. In part, this American dilemma was of their own making, since it contained all the complicated issues they had raised of confidence and trust—issues that were basically matters of psychology.

But for a time American attitudes to Western Europe continued to reflect a misinterpretation of this essential political element in US strategic policy-making. It was conceived in Washington that Europeans needed a greater role in making the decisions governing the use of nuclear weapons, in order to quiet fears that the United States would abandon the Continent in a crisis. This was a view that accorded well with much thinking on the Continent, particularly in West Germany, where the prospect of losing the American nuclear guarantee was most frightening.

In the American approach the problem of emphasis was placed, not so much on reaching a new political understanding with the West Europeans, as on prescribing the creation of actual weapons that the Europeans could 'have', and thereby feel that they were taking part in the West's nuclear deterrent. In theory, the credibility of the US nuclear deterrent would be enhanced—in the eyes of the European Allies—if the latter had some say in Western nuclear policy. Independent deterrents, of course, were still suspect in Washington: they were too small, too vulnerable, and too likely to frighten the Russians into doing something rash.

The so-called 'hardware' solution to the so-called 'nuclear sharing' problem—this fascinating exercise in diplomatic gymnastics—began rather early, with a proposal in December 1960 by the Eisenhower Administration to earmark US *Polaris* submarines for NATO. And this proposal was put into practice in 1963 when three of the US submarines were assigned to NATO for planning purposes. Of course, the conceit was transparent: the nuclear warheads would never be fired without the permission of SACEUR, who, himself, had to receive the necessary command not from the North Atlantic Council, but, as with all NATO nuclear weapons, except a few British ones (even those US tactical and so-called 'interdiction' weapons stationed with Allied forces), from the President of the United States.

This was not the only American effort to resolve the problem of nuclear 'credibility'—an effort that no European for a moment took seriously. There has also been an arrangement since 1963 whereby a certain number of NATO officers have been permitted to take part in the planning process of the Americans at the headquarters of the Strategic Air Command in Omaha, Nebraska, where targets for nuclear attack are selected. But equally, this step involves no influence for Europeans on the use of the weapons themselves.

This effort was little noted at the time, but seems in retrospect to have had more merit, in terms of creating patterns of political co-operation, than was granted to it—as will become clear in the following discussion of the so-called Nuclear Planning Group.

But the big effort by the Americans to resolve their dilemma was to follow, in a proposal that lived and died at least twice. This was a proposal for a fleet of ships equipped with *Polaris* missiles, with the ships being under the command of SACEUR and manned by men from as many NATO countries as wished to take part. This was the Multilateral Force, the most ludicrous of a host of NATO eccentricities, and which was the product of a small group of men in the American State and Navy Departments, who were once aptly referred to as 'a tidy-minded group of fanatics' for their failure to reconcile the logic of their case with the facts of European political and psychological attitudes.

In any event, this group of supporters for the 'MLF', as the project came to be called, won the day from time to time within the American government; and over a period of more than two years, West European governments were submitted to varying degrees of pressure to adopt the proposal. Many did, though largely because of this pressure from Washington, which was not the way in which the project had been conceived at all. The idea had been that Europeans should be reassured by the MLF, not dragooned into accepting it as a way of showing their loyalty to American leadership of the Western Alliance. Plans were drawn up; a ship was commissioned; it was filled with a multi-national crew. Special cooks and foods were provided, facilities for separate religious observance were laid on, and a great show was made of the value of 'mixed-manning'.

But the central issue was continually evaded. Who would be able to fire the missiles with their nuclear warheads? And how important would the MLF be in the Western deterrent strategy since it was Lilliputian in comparison with the American strategic arsenal? The answers were clear: the Americans would retain custody of the nuclear warheads, and the force would really be rather insignificant. Yet the Americans made a promise, which reflected still another underlying characteristic of the whole history of NATO: if the Europeans somehow managed to forge among themselves a measure of *political* unity, then control of the MLF warheads could be turned over to them, as part of the so-called 'twin pillars' (or 'dumb-bell') approach to the concept of 'Atlantic partnership'. This is a subject worthy of extended discussion—particularly since the American penchant for European political unity has had such an important role in the shaping of NATO—and will be discussed at length in Chapter 5.

Of course, for the simple reason that such unity was premature at best, and visionary at worst, this American offer to transfer control of the nuclear warheads for the MLF was never taken up by the Europeans, and the whole project fell into increasing disrepute. Even those countries which had agreed to participate felt somehow that this mechanical approach was no way to solve the *political* problems of consultation and confidence within an Alliance. But this point was not appreciated in Washington—nor the 'hardware' approach abandoned—until considerable damage had been done to the relations among Allies. Ironically, American domination of the Alliance was most apparent at the very moment—and through the very agency—that the Americans were using to try to cope with the problem of that dominance.

As with the earlier dilemma posed by the need for rearmament of West Germany, which had led to the proposal for a Western European Union in 1954, a way out of the MLF debate was provided by the British Government. In the autumn of 1964, the new Labour Government proposed an alternative to the MLF, to be called the Atlantic Nuclear Force, a scheme to be based on existing deterrents. Suddenly the context of debate was broadened from the old one requiring a stand either for or against the MLF, and other nations were given scope to try ending the whole search for a 'hardware' approach to solve political problems. By this time, of course, the prophecy made by the supporters of the MLF had largely been fulfilled, and there was, indeed, a 'German nuclear problem'—i.e. a growing desire in the Federal Republic for greater assurances concerning the US nuclear guarantee—though it is impossible to tell whether there would have been such a problem, anyway. But President Johnson rightly concluded that the MLF was not the right road to anywhere, and quietly buried the project.

So, with the demise of the MLF, the Alliance was faced with a true dilemma; there appeared to be a real need for some means of solving the problems of nuclear sharing, and especially to establish West Germany's place in it, yet there was no obvious approach to take that did not raise as many problems as it solved.

In the event, the solution proved to be relatively simple: at Mr McNamara's suggestion, the interested nations of Western Europe joined together in discussions that gave the Allies a real sense of participation, not in any 'hardware' solution to the sharing of nuclear weapons, but rather in working through the actual problems faced by the Americans as principal custodians of the NATO nuclear deterrent. Out of this process there developed in December 1966 a Nuclear Planning Group of 7 nations[1] that almost miraculously seemed to put the nuclear sharing problems more or less to rest. All at once, the issue of the decade had largely evaporated—an issue which had taken the Allies through the agonizing boredom of the MLF debates which themselves showed that the Alliance was stronger than was often believed, since it survived this shock largely intact in political terms. This was the lesson derived from the three-year-old practice of sending NATO officers to Omaha. It seemed to work for the Alliance as a whole.

Yet this explanation is all rather too simple. Again, one must look at the development of events outside the limited NATO context. Following the Cuban Missile Crisis of 1962—one might even say following the last of the Berlin 'crises' in 1961, and the building of the mutually convenient Berlin Wall—the political air began to clear throughout Europe and in Russian-American

[1] Membership rotates among the Allies, but in practice West Germany, the United Kingdom, and the United States are always members, while Greece and Turkey alternate in sharing one of the other seats.

relations. The awful risks taken by both nations over Cuba became obvious to all; it was equally clear that such risks were intolerable for so little potential gain.

Almost immediately, the political climate between East and West improved; and in August 1963, a treaty to end the testing of nuclear weapons in the air, underwater, and in outer space, was signed at last. Of course, there were many factors working towards this new spirit of *détente*—factors that will be discussed in more detail in a final chapter, and which included the onset of strategic stability that entailed the mutual acquisition of second-strike deterrents; the recognition that the borders of Europe had remained stable for 15 years; and the psychological impact of the Cuban Missile Crisis itself.

But within Europe itself, the most important effect of this process was the gradual recognition that the context of military confrontation, begun so many years before, had just about worked out its own internal logic. NATO was widely believed to be relatively equal in terms of military power with the nations of the Warsaw Pact—although, as noted earlier, the perception of this development depended on certain specific assumptions about the nature of warfare in Europe; second, there was a clear and recognized division of the Continent which could serve as a basis on which to conduct a form of bargaining between East and West. Gradually, it became possible for governments to raise their heads above the parapets, and see how the world had changed. Down at NATO Headquarters, bureaucrats and military officers still viewed matters within the same logic of their narrow context—and some still do as this book is written in 1969; but outside these narrow confines and those, perhaps, obtaining within the military structure of the Warsaw Pact, there appeared to be some scope for looking beyond the limits of Cold War to appreciate the possibilities of actually *changing* patterns of confrontation—and patterns of economic and political behaviour—throughout the Continent.

The debate over the MLF ended at just about the same time that the new spirit in Europe—the new basis for the relaxing of tensions—was becoming truly apparent. Therefore, when the Nuclear Planning Group was proposed, it proved to be the needed political effort to 'solve' the problem of nuclear sharing. After all, within the new context of relaxed tensions (*détente*), where the prospect of war was seen to be receding further every day, there seemed to be less urgency in considering the actual fighting of wars, or even of being certain about the process of deterring them. For most Europeans at least—and this included many West Germans as well as a growing number of Americans —the prospects were not of war, but of the coming of a more or less permanent peace and the possibility of changes in existing patterns of confrontation in Europe. It was as though the MLF were the last exercise in which many of the Allies were willing to bury their heads in the sands of the old context of military confrontation, and in doing so, to abide by the rules of that limited game, instead of looking outside to see how the world was changing.

And, as the context of confrontation seemed to change— however slightly—so did the strategy of the Western Alliance and even, according to some observers, the strategy of the Warsaw Pact as well, as the central role of nuclear weapons in the latter's strategy was gradually modified. First, there was a change on the part of France; then on the part of the NATO Alliance itself.

The major change in the French attitude came in February 1966, and it was presented in one of the well-rehearsed press conferences of President de Gaulle. In the first place, he emphasised his view that the external threat to the Alliance had decreased rapidly—an observation that undoubtedly re-presented the basic motivation behind his words, but which was more or less lost on those Alliance members who were struggling to maintain the cohesive facade of the Alliance. Because of their urgent institutional pre-occupation, they were prone to ignore the profound changes then taking place on the Continent: i.e. changes in the direction of a gradual dissolution of at least the non-military aspects of confrontation.

It was in this context that de Gaulle noted the classic argument about American vulnerability to Soviet nuclear attack—discussed earlier—and said that the use of American nuclear weapons on Europe's behalf had become uncertain (see Appendix IV). This, for France, had removed the justification there had been for continuing with the integration of French military forces within Allied Command Europe, but not, he was careful to stress—and few outsiders listened to this qualification—for the Alliance itself. On the other hand, there was the other half of his argument: that integration also meant that conflicts involving the US in other parts of the world might draw Europe automatically into a wider conflict. The emphasis was on the idea of 'automatic', and it was certainly true that the integration of forces within NATO was of such a nature as to make the right of national decision in the event of an actual war not very meaningful. Therefore, the costs of alliance had gone up, at the very moment that the benefits had gone down. And, furthermore, France was in the process of acquiring atomic bombs, and had a new-found opportunity—as well as the will—to be responsible for her own destiny.

The practical consequences of this act—which in de Gaulle's words re-established a 'normal situation of sovereignty'—were not long in coming: the Allied Commands were required to depart from the soil of France, as were all American and Canadian forces stationed there. French forces were withdrawn from Allied Command Europe—although, in a special agreement concluded with the West Germans, who were less inclined to be purists about the sanctity of the NATO integrated command than they were about their relations with France, it was agreed that France's two divisions should remain stationed in the German Federal Republic.

Then the acrimony began, with the Americans revealing several previously secret treaties about the stationing of forces, which France was supposed to be violating by its *démarche*. France was told bluntly that she would have to pay for the whole move and for the real estate being left behind. The French Government refused. And some rather strange ideas were touted, including a proposal to place a communications satellite high over the NATO area, thereby eliminating France's physical importance to NATO communications.

At the same time, the Allies prepared for the move from France, and immediately saw this as an opportunity to 'streamline' Allied Command Europe, in order to make it conform to the ideal principles of the way a command structure should be run. This 'streamlining' was accomplished with dispatch, and the two expelled military commands were relocated in the Netherlands (Allied Forces Central Europe) and at Casteau, in Belgium (SHAPE). Within a year, France's formal links with the integrated command structure of NATO had been effectively dissolved.

At first, the blow struck by the French at the fabric of the Alliance and of its strategy seemed a severe one. But subsequently a cooler view prevailed. It soon appeared that, in actual combat terms, the loss of the two French divisions hardly mattered at all to Allied Command Europe, since NATO strategy would have required an escalation to a nuclear phase of warfare before these French troops, lying well back from the Czech frontier, had even been engaged in combat. French attack aircraft were lost to SACEUR, but French air defences continued to be integrated with those of the rest of the Allies. Supply lines had to be re-routed away from France, and became more vulnerable to enemy attack, and air space over France has no longer been automatically available for training purposes. But all in all, there has been very little strategic loss to Allied Command Europe occasioned by the departure of the French contingents from SACEUR's command.

Why, then, was there all the fuss, particularly at a time when there was a gradual loosening of NATO ties as more governments perceived a radical reduction in the Soviet threat? The answer lies in the problems that the Allies were having in trying to construct something more out of the Alliance than just an expedient mechanism for combating a specific threat.

There was, quite simply, no clear idea of how to convert the process of confrontation in Europe—the 'logic' of which was rapidly working itself through to a conclusion—into something else in which NATO and the Warsaw Pact did not occupy the central positions in ordering strategic relations among European nations. And, faced with this prospect, most of the NATO Allies found that preserving an existing security arrangement was essential to the process of developing alternative arrangements, as well as being necessary to preserve the appearance in the meantime that the NATO Alliance was as viable strategically and politically as it had ever been.

Strategically, therefore, in 1966 de Gaulle really did little *to* the Alliance. But he did much *for* it politically, in the sense that he focused attention on the obvious strains—particularly those related to American dominance—and on the difficulties involved in changing the pattern of confrontation across the whole of Europe. He was, in effect, requiring NATO's officials and national leaders to come to terms with the problems that they had been unable—or unwilling—to handle; and he did it in circumstances that dramatized that need, and perhaps even overdid it.

The further development of this point really relates to the specific problems of *détente*, which will be discussed in the final chapter. Yet it is worth noting here the intimate connection between NATO's strategic posture and the political relations within the Alliance at every period in the Alliance's history. In 1966 de Gaulle at least *seemed* to change some of the strategic understandings of the Alliance, and thus began a process of strategic change within the Alliance, which—although many Allies complained with some justification that it had been delayed by French intransigence—began to come to grips with some of the changes in the problems of European confrontation and security: changes which had been delayed since the last Berlin crisis of 1961, and the Cuban missile crisis of 1962.

Within months of the final adjustments brought about by the French *démarche*, the strategy of the NATO Alliance was changed in noticeable ways, and, at the same time, the Allies removed the North Atlantic Council from Paris—unasked—on the grounds that close 'co-ordination' was needed between it and SHAPE, despite the fact that this step had the effect of isolating France further within the Alliance. The Allies also reactivated the Defence Planning Committee (DPC) of the North Atlantic Council in order to keep France from being privy to military secrets that would otherwise have been shared in common in the Council. And, in May 1967, the DPC gave new 'political, strategic, and economic guidance' to NATO's military planners. This meant two important changes to NATO's strategy. In the first place, the final adjustment was made on the long-standing political debate whether to plan NATO's defences on the basis of Soviet military *capabilities* as opposed to their political *intentions*. In 1967, the Allies decided that interpretations of the latter could be given much greater weight, in view of an obvious reduction in the Soviet 'threat' occasioned by *détente* and the perception that the confrontation across the Continent had now become genuinely stable. This was, in effect, an admission that war in Europe was unlikely, and that the retention of NATO in its present form depended as much upon failure to find ways of providing alternative means of European security, as on anything else. There was some modification of this view following the Soviet invasion of Czechoslovakia in August 1968, but the distinction between Soviet 'intentions' and 'capabilities' was even then not again entirely blurred.

The second change was related to the first: that the Allies believed war would not come in Europe without adequate 'political warning time' that would permit Allied defences to be brought up to the level required to cope with any plausible threat, at least on the Central Front. This change was even more profound than the first, since it represented not only the availability of sophisticated means to detect troop movements in Eastern Europe, but also a philosophical acceptance in the West of the intimate connection between political conflict and military threat, and an acceptance that the two contexts have real and significant interactions. It was a fundamental indication of the progress of *détente*. It meant equally that the gap in what could be called a 'philosophy of conflict', as between the Russians and the Americans, had narrowed so significantly as to make possible real political understandings between East and West, despite the continued, but less meaningful, context of military confrontation on the Continent.

These changes in attitude within NATO reflected more than just changes in the perception of Soviet political attitudes; as with all of NATO's strategic problems, the acceptance of 'political warning time' reflected the economic needs of member states. Of course, one might argue that the willingness of nations to undertake expenditure on defence is at least relevant to judging their real belief about the nature of the potential threat, whatever the political rhetoric of their statesmen. In this case, balance of payments difficulties, especially in Britain and America, increased the domestic pressures on governments to re-evaluate and minimize the Soviet threat, and, with it, NATO's response. The long discussions within NATO on offset-cost payments (discussed in Chapter 3) influenced official perceptions of threat and response. Indeed, as discussed earlier, by the beginning of 1968 the Americans were even able to contend—though not without contradiction—that NATO countries on the Central Front actually had available to them, in terms relevant to a potential conflict, more forces than were available to Warsaw Pact commanders—i.e. NATO could implement the doctrine of a form of flexible response then recently adopted—assuming that no war would last long enough for there to be major reinforcements from the Soviet Union.

The decisions taken within the North Atlantic Council to accept the criterion of intentions as well as that of capabilities for determining threat and response, and to accept the existence of 'political warning time', meant that a number of troops could be withdrawn from the Central Front. 5,000 men were returned home to the United Kingdom, and 35,000 to the United States. In theory, these troops were only being 'redeployed'—that is, they could be returned to Europe in the event of a crisis. In actual fact, they represented real troop reductions which, taken together, potentially had a greater strategic impact on the Alliance than did the withdrawal of France's two divisions from Allied Command Europe, French divisions which, of course, were not withdrawn from the Federal Republic of Germany itself.

Significantly, there was no outcry on the Continent about all these moves; no anxiety that fewer troops would mean a weakening of the American nuclear commitment and no onset of a new 'nuclear sharing' problem. Thus *détente* reduced still further the strategic problems facing the Allies, and, with it, the political rationale for keeping the Alliance together. This development was recognized, and the results—culminating in the so-called Harmel Study—will be discussed in Chapter 5. Of course, it would be rash to discount a recurrence of some of these 'pre-*détente*' problems within the NATO Alliance, particularly if there is a further divergence between US and West European attitudes concerning the proper means for approaching problems of change in Europe in concert with the Soviet Union and her East European Allies. In particular, the trauma in the US over possible disengagement from Vietnam has raised again—in muted form—European fears of a new American isolationism and, with it, the prospect of a new form of the old 'nuclear sharing' problem.

There has been one further modification to NATO strategy that is worthy of note here. In August 1968—following long deliberations within NATO about further steps in pursuit of *détente* and even proposals from the Eastern bloc about finding ways of dissolving both NATO and the Warsaw Pact—there came the invasion of Czechoslovakia by the Soviet Union.

The initial reaction of many observers was that the strategic balance had been altered in Europe. This was the view put forward by the American Secretary of State, perhaps more to obscure the real bases of *détente* as he had understood them— *viz.* the tacit acceptance of 'spheres of influence' in Europe, despite their unacceptability within the terms of American political rhetoric—than for any reason of considered judgement (see Chapter 6). In fact, it was quickly accepted that the presence of extra Soviet divisions on NATO's eastern boundary did not seem to upset the actual strategic balance in Europe, since these troops faced mountains in South Germany that were secured primarily by US forces. The really vulnerable areas on NATO's Central Front remained those embracing the northern plains; and the Russians had clearly acquired a number of strategic liabilities with their alienation of the whole nation of Czechoslovakia—at the very least, none of the more than 14 Czech divisions could any longer effectively be counted in the Warsaw Pact Order of Battle.

But the truly remarkable phenomenon was the limited reaction on the part of the NATO Allies after they had had time to consider the situation; even at the time, NATO forces did not go on alert status. There was later some pressure to increase troops levels of West European states—pressures exerted largely by the Americans—as well as token increases by Great Britain and one or two lesser Allies. But beyond these half-hearted measures there were no radical transformations. Even more remarkable, perhaps, was the fact that, in all the new talk about force levels, the so-called nuclear question was only reintroduced obliquely by the British Defence Secretary, and even then there has been no wide-scale revival of the pressing anxieties in Europe about the US nuclear guarantee— although it was clear that NATO lacked the forces actually to put into operation its official (though obscure) doctrine of a form of 'flexible response'.

Détente was definitely impaired, at least from the standpoint of the Western Europeans. But in the process, there was no automatic re-establishment of a rigid context of military confrontation. It was as though, once the period of anxiety of the Cold War had passed, it could not return—the mould had been broken; the understandings reached with the East over the years on strategic matters would not disappear in spite of violations of certain rules of thumb on more political and economic matters—e.g. the increasingly free relations between Eastern and Western European countries. This was definitely a firm sign that the end of military confrontation was at hand, provided that some means could be found to convert confrontation into an alternative means of providing security.

At the present time, no such scheme has gained widespread acceptance, although many have been canvassed (see Chapter 6).

During this period of *détente* the Allies' strategic preoccupations have really concentrated on matters extraneous to the problems of fighting a war on the Central Front—though the French, who have been trying to define an independent role within the context of NATO, have shown more interest in strategic problems, particularly as regards the *force de dissuasion* and the concept of 'proportional deterrence'. For the rest, there has remained concern lest the Russians be tempted to achieve a *fait accompli* in northern reaches of Norway ('Finnmark') or the eastern lands of Turkey—concerns more psychological than strategic. And the NATO Allies have been still more concerned lest the increasing Soviet fleet in the Mediterranean should provide strategic—as well as political—problems. This concern has been particularly acute when measured in terms of threats to the flank areas and the question of Alliance cohesion (see Chapter 5). Indeed, in November 1968, the Allies established a new command to keep watch over the Soviet Mediterranean fleet—Maritime Air Forces Mediterranean; earlier in the year the British had agreed to commit some extra ships to the Mediterranean; and even the French seemed interested in the problem.

But at this point, the strategic interests of the NATO Allies seemed to be concentrated, not so much on actual military threats, as on the problems posed for the distribution of influence within the Alliance, as preparations were continually discussed for transforming the pattern of military confrontation. In addition, the focus was concentrated on the increasingly divergent interests of America and her European Allies. As with other matters of *détente*, these issues involved the question of whether or not the United States would be able to proceed to reach limited understandings with the Soviet Union over the heads of her Allies. Therefore, there was considerable concern about the negotiation of the nuclear Non-Proliferation Treaty, which many Europeans chose, not without reason, to see in the light of US-Soviet and US-Western European relations. Here, the 'German problem' was not so much one of the Bonn Government's needing nuclear weapons—or even guarantees—for defence and deterrence, as it was of the West Germans' wishing to have a veto on possible US-Soviet arrangements for Europe. This was, in effect, a form of Gaullism.

This is a cursory analysis of some of the strategic problems facing the North Atlantic Alliance over the years. These are not all the strategic problems that are usually discussed—such as infinitely boring and virtually irrelevant problems like those related to tactical nuclear weapons. But they are the essential questions more related to the manner in which strategic problems illuminate the political relations within the Alliance. This construction is used deliberately, instead of the one that would seem to be important—i.e. the relations between East and West. For over the years, the strategic problems of NATO seem to have related more directly to the processes of bargaining within NATO—and to adjustments in internal influence—than to changes in the actual pattern of confrontation with the Soviet Union. Of course, there were significant changes between East and West. But it is reasonable to ask to what extent the changes of perception in the West about Soviet intentions and capabilities were valid representations of changes actually taking place in the East. To what extent were changes that were perceived in the relations between East and West based on information that could be verified, and to what extent on new expectations both in the West and the East—based, perhaps, even on wish fulfilment? Finally, to what extent did the establishment of a military context of confrontation impose a logic that had to be worked through and, only then, permit radical reappraisals to be made of the conditions that were believed to have established the context in the first place?

Some of these questions are being answered, at least in part, in the course of this discussion. At least one can certainly see the way in which strategic debates and the political climate within the NATO Alliance interacted with one another. But other aspects of the same phenomenon must also be examined: in this case the way in which those functions proposed for or adopted by NATO—functions not related directly to military confrontation—also affected the development of the Alliance. In the process, these functions also had a major bearing on questions of European security.

Chapter 5

Non-Military Roles of the Alliances

In order to understand the progress of European security since the Second World War, one must go far beyond a simple analysis of the construction and operation of NATO; beyond an analysis of threats and responses; beyond a discussion of strategy; and beyond a consideration of the role of the Warsaw Pact in Eastern Europe. There must also be some discussion of the non-military aspects of Alliances—particularly those of NATO, where the process of super-power domination was most clearly channelled through the military institution throughout the life of the Alliance.

From the very beginning, important non-security matters were involved in the formation of a Western security institution —matters that had profound importance, not only for the nature of that security, but also for the political and economic future of Western Europe, of US-European relations, and of the prospects for altering the basic pattern of East-West confrontation.

To begin with, in 1948 the British Foreign Secretary, Ernest Bevin, proposed the formation of an alliance of several West European states, beginning with Britain, France, and the Benelux states—i.e. a Western Union. At that time there were strong feelings, particularly among people and statesmen on the Continent, that this approach should be used to form the basis of more comprehensive political and economic arrangements. During the course of presenting his ideas, Bevin managed to give his new European allies the impression that the British Government was also interested in these matters, and this impression still found some support on the Continent two years later and was reinforced by Winston Churchill's leadership in

Britain of the European unity movement. It is not the purpose of this study to demonstrate whether or not subsequent British aloofness from involvement in Continental moves towards political and economic integration was the result of deliberate policy in 1948. But there was certainly a considerable display of unhappiness by Continental statesmen when the British later showed themselves to be less than 'good Europeans'—itself a political shibboleth of the 1950s and early 1960s. At the same time, the British themselves were certainly presented with a series of difficult dilemmas, as they attempted to reconcile their involvements on the Continent both with their commitments to the Commonwealth and with their hankering to establish and maintain a 'special relationship' with their giant neighbour across the Atlantic.

In any event, the Brussels Treaty Organization, which was established in March 1948 to embody the institutional aspects of this Western Union, carried considerable political and economic potential. Indeed, for at least the four European members of Western Union—France, Belgium, the Netherlands, and Luxembourg—these aspects were as important as those military ones which gained so much attention following the Czech *coup* and the beginning of the Berlin blockade.

This European interest in political and economic co-operation was reflected in the nature of the organization set up under the treaty—even though the treaty was largely negotiated after the *coup* in Prague. Among other things, it established a Consultative Council that, in practice, involved consultations among national finance ministers as well as among those responsible for military and foreign political affairs. The finance ministers interpreted their brief in very broad terms, and in their deliberations covered issues going far beyond what would be expected in a traditional military alliance or, indeed, far beyond what came to be the practice in NATO itself.

This was understandable. After all, these European nations were in the midst of a complex process of forming a comprehensive set of institutions among themselves to cover matters such as a customs union. Indeed, at the beginning of 1948, the Benelux Union was becoming a reality, with the establishment of a customs union and the unification of external tariffs, and the French were actively engaged in negotiations with Italy to establish a customs union of their own. Within the year, active discussions were also on foot about a merger of the two schemes to be called by the unattractive term 'Fritilux', while to the north the Scandinavian states began talking of a similar project, to be called 'Danosve'.

Partly because of their interest in these projects of economic co-operation, the European nations in Western Union had as one of their principal concerns the desire to keep their new venture tightly-knit and free from competing focuses of attention, in order to preserve the potential benefits Western Union could provide in moving all of them in the direction of greater European integration. The flaw, of course, lay in the attitude of Great Britain, which moved increasingly towards Atlantic ties that were later widely seen on the Continent to be, almost by their very nature, incompatible with the most profound of European involvements—namely, full political union. Accordingly, during the period of discussion leading up to the establishment of an Atlantic Pact, British attention swung round to the possibility of getting the best of all possible worlds: America, Europe, and the Commonwealth. This was the so-called 'three circles' policy that was pursued in different forms by several British Governments for more than a decade.

These considerations were important in the development both of European security arrangements and of relations across the emerging division between East and West. This was so because the character of Western European political and economic interests played a significant role in the whole history of NATO's development, not only as a security organization, but also as a focus of moves towards European integration.

This process long had the strong support of various United States Administrations and the Congress, which saw a United States of Europe as possibly the best means of avoiding further fratricidal conflicts on the Continent, like the wars of 1914–18 and 1939–45 in which the Americans had reluctantly been led to take part. Indeed, the establishment of a Western Union in the first place owed much to the American Government's desire that the Europeans take concrete steps towards political and economic integration before Marshall aid would be provided. Thus, partly in the interest of advancing this integration, the Brussels Treaty Organization was brought into being; in turn, it helped to institutionalize the Cold War and to bring into sharper relief both the division of Europe and the concrete forms of this division, including Russia's network of bilateral treaties in Eastern Europe.

There was concern among the four West European members of Western Union to protect their efforts at achieving economic and political integration from being dissipated; this concern was reflected in the process of forming the wider alliance, NATO. Basically, the question was which nations should be invited to take part? The Western Union countries felt strongly that the new alliance designed to bridge the Atlantic should be limited to the original five countries, plus the United States and Canada; at least these limits should be fixed until the Brussels Treaty Organization was assured of preserving its integrity. This would have been the best of all possible worlds: there would be guarantees from across the Atlantic to provide a foundation for economic recovery, while Western Union would be preserved as a basis for further political and economic efforts. Nor was this an idle concept; after all, this period in European development—from 1948 to about 1952—was one of the most creative periods in the Continent's history, when it is viewed from the standpoint of new institutions and new approaches to solve old problems. From its inception, Western Union was widely seen to be a central part of this process, and it was thought to be worth preserving, however great the need for firm commitments from the Americans and possibly also their direct involvement in Continental affairs.

Almost immediately, there appeared a conflict of interest,

one which had significant implications for the structure of confrontation as well as for the political and economic development of Western Europe. The American Government's enthusiasm for European integration led it to tie together virtually every step towards providing aid and security, beginning with the Marshall Plan, with political developments on the Continent. The Americans—including the Secretary of State and Senate leaders—wanted some grand conception to be based upon the 16 Marshall Plan countries. Therefore, for this reason as well as to provide security on an 'efficient' and co-ordinated basis, the Americans favoured a broadening of the North Atlantic conception. For example, there was considerable reluctance in Washington to see the Nordic powers in Scandinavia develop a form of security organization on their own, separate from the one which the Americans envisaged in Western Europe. The prospect of a Nordic Pact was seen in Washington to diminish the prospects for wider West European integration, as, indeed, it would have done. As a result, the Americans put some pressure on these countries to join the new, wider conception, by declaring that no pact of which the US was not a member—i.e. any but the emerging Atlantic Pact— would receive the military aid that the others could expect.

From the American point of view, this stand made some sense, as it also did when viewed from the standpoint of running an efficient system of foreign aid and of forging a strong bulwark in Western Europe to meet what the Americans saw as the Soviet threat. But both of these views presupposed that an immutable confrontation already existed; that it had to be seen in military terms; and that the best way of dealing with it was to eliminate all traces of ambiguity throughout Western Europe. Consequently, the Swedes found it necessary to abandon consideration of any form of Scandinavian security organization in order to preserve what, for them, was an ambiguity more essential and valuable for their defence than could be any guarantee from the Americans or participation in a North Atlantic Alliance. Ironically, the Swedes had actively considered joining Western Union and had been impressed by its economic and political possibilities as opposed to the military ones that eventually came to dominate it.

A similar view obtained in Norway, but the Norwegians did eventually join the discussions being held with regard to the formation of a North Atlantic treaty, after the Russians provided Oslo with a convenient rationale by putting diplomatic pressure on the Norwegian Government to stand aloof. This was just another example of Soviet obtuseness, leading to the opposite result from that intended; and yet the West continued to credit the Russians with perfection in intrigue and in the manoeuvres of diplomacy.

Three years later, there was a development in NATO similar to the American pressure on the Scandinavians to join the wider Alliance. In 1952, Greece and Turkey joined the twelve-member Alliance, not so much because there was any strategic rationale for their doing so—they were hardly linked to the European Central Front—but rather because this step helped them to share in the common sense of cohesion and purpose. It may be argued that bilateral American guarantees to these latter two countries would have been more effective— as would, perhaps, even a Mediterranean-American security pact—but at the time there was the strongest sense in the United States that the Soviet threat should be regarded as indivisible: if any one 'Western' nation were attacked, all would be at risk.

In both these cases—US pressure *against* a Nordic Pact and *for* a pact including the eastern Mediterranean powers—the process itself helped to solidify the East-West division and formalize the military nature of confrontation. And in this process considerable room was lost for diplomatic manoeuvre and for excluding some areas from the scope of confrontation— as happened with Sweden and later with Austria. Of course, this view assumes that there did indeed exist some room for diplomatic manoeuvre in 1949: a moot point.

But in early 1949, as the Atlantic Treaty was being discussed, the process of including outside states went even further, partly for parochial reasons. If the integrity of Western Union was to be breached at the outset, then France wanted Italy to be included, largely in view of Franco-Italian *rapprochement* and the discussions on a customs union, even though this step entailed some real compromises for the new Alliance in view of Italy's status as a defeated Axis power. Britain wanted Norway, partly because of the close ties evolved long before the Second World War, and also Portugal, with the ancient and honourable treaty of 1373—the oldest surviving treaty of alliance in Britain's collection.

The inclusion of Italy suited the Americans—who had already made some pledges which it would be easier to redeem inside the same Alliance—and they were pleased with the prospect of having Portugal, in order to use the air bases established in the Azores during the war, although they agreed that no troops would be stationed there in time of peace.

Should there be more? Indeed there should: Denmark decided to join, partly at least, in order to regain some control over portions of Greenland that the Americans had been using since the war as bases. By broadening the context of these agreements to the form of a multilateral alliance, the Danes ran less of a risk of trouble in coping with a super-Ally. And Iceland joined, also partly, at least, because of the anomalous status of foreign forces which had to all intents and purposes occupied the island during the war.

Two countries, however, were left out—to say nothing of the western part of Germany, which was still in a particularly anomalous position in Europe. These were Ireland and Spain. The former offered to join if Britain were excluded. As for Spain, the Americans argued loud and long for its inclusion— over the bitter opposition of the rest of the Allies—until President Truman himself intervened on the side of the liberal Democrats in Congress. But Spain was later admitted to NATO by the back door, as it were, in the form of bilateral agreements made with Washington and with the provision of enough economic aid and payments for the rental on US bases in Spain to underwrite its economic development.

Thus NATO became, not a seven-nation alliance, but a twelve-nation one, and would eventually become one of fifteen. The nature of confrontation was broadened, and those ambiguities remaining in Europe were discounted for the sake of efficiency and a better chance for a real defence and system of guarantees. This was not necessarily a bad choice, although it proved somewhat limiting diplomatically in later years, to say nothing of the problems, which were thus exacerbated, of maintaining Alliance 'cohesion', of finding ways to co-ordinate Alliance policies on *détente*, and of reassuring outlying Allies— Norway and Turkey—against a possible Russian 'snatch and grab' attack.

Despite the size of the new alliance, the Brussels Treaty Powers tried to preserve the sense of their own organization until, at least, the British found their Atlantic ties to be more desirable than the prospect of submerging their sovereignty in some wild and woolly European venture. Indeed, the Western Union Defence Organization and all of its appurtenances were not completely subsumed under NATO until the end of 1951, and even then the semblance of political organization was retained and then broadened to become the Western European Union (WEU) after the Germans and Italians acceded to the Brussels Treaty in late 1954. Indeed, at the time of the 20th anniversary of NATO, there was still talk of using this framework of WEU to co-ordinate the policies of Western European nations, as distinct from those policies arrived at with the United States. This was an approach that was also implicit in the idea of a 'European Caucus' within NATO.

But, in 1949, the rudimentary structure of Western Union was unable to retain its zest in the face of the overriding demands of the developing relationship with America, and of the heavy emphasis of the new Alliance on military matters. In consequence, soon after NATO came into being, the Continental members of Western Union began to follow other courses, beginning with the Schuman Plan for a European Coal and Steel Community (ECSC). For reasons alluded to above, the British did not accede to the ECSC as it was set up in 1950-2, but there were six countries to take part: these were the nucleus of Western Union, which included France and the three Benelux countries, plus Italy and West Germany. This was a significant list. In part, it was a recognition that the division of Europe (and of Germany) had been institutionalized to such an extent that there was little to be lost in terms of future diplomatic 'movement' with the Russians on the issue of Germany by including the Federal Republic in an economic scheme which was envisaged merely as the first step towards 'functional' integration —i.e. integration proceeding area by area—and eventual political and economic union.

But there was another, more strategic, significance behind the ECSC and the European Movement in general. This process also indicated that the Americans and, to an extent, the British, had not taken seriously enough the real fears felt by the four Continental members of Western Union that there could be a resurgence of military threat from a revived Germany. In theory, the ECSC would make war 'impossible' by tying up the basic resources of war—iron, coal and steel— in a supranational context that would give no single nation the power to launch another major European war. In the nuclear age, such an assumption may be inadequate, but at least this rationale which was provided for the joint efforts made by these six nations did indicate the widespread fear of a resurgent Germany that could once again threaten the security of Europe. Indeed, it is interesting to note that the Russians never opposed this move towards Western European integration to the same degree that they opposed either the less encompassing Marshall Plan, the inclusion of West Germany in NATO, or the defensive component of West European integration— namely, the ill-fated European Defence Community (EDC). The major point at issue with all these efforts, as far as the Russians were concerned, was the possibility of a revived

German threat; and moves towards what was clearly West European integration set the Russians a problem of conflicting objectives: they were against further progress towards consolidating and strengthening Western Europe, but they were also in favour of containing German power.

It was the next step in European integration after the ECSC —in part also an effort to find a place for Germany that would settle fears about it—that brought the strategic problems to the fore. This effort reflected the complex issue that centred on the best way of providing West German forces to implement NATO's 'forward strategy', but without creating a truly national West German Army.

The solution seemed to lie in the Pleven Plan, which proposed an extension of the concept of functional integration into the realm of defence and, by implication, eventually into the strictly political realm through a politically unified European community. West Germany would take part in this new European Defence Community as an equal partner with the other five members, and would be allowed to rearm; but there would be no question of re-establishing a German General Staff, nor of permitting German units to operate on their own. Within European parliaments, there was some debate about the size of units that should be permitted to be 'all-German', above which point all commands would be organized on a supranational basis. But the principle was clear: no independent fighting capability should be returned to Germany, and her troops were to be firmly subordinated to an international command. This arrangement, in turn, was to be made an adjunct of NATO, and thereby would be firmly committed to it.

Needless to say, this proposal for an EDC brought the stiffest opposition from the Russians, although it was undoubtedly less provocative to them, and was apparently seen as such by Moscow, if one compares its reactions during the period of discussion on the EDC with its reactions later when West Germany joined NATO. The Russians threatened to establish a military

Alliance of their own in Eastern Europe if the latter step were taken; and they duly carried out their threat.

The debate on the EDC continued until August 1954, and included the signing of the treaty and its ratification by five of the six signatories. But then the French National Assembly rejected the agreement and it collapsed. There were many reasons for this, but the decisive one, perhaps, was not so much the failure of Britain to adhere to EDC as a growing reaction in France against the pace of European integration and the necessary merging of sovereignties that that process entailed. The establishment of common sovereignty in the crucial sphere of defence, as opposed to the limited economic sphere of coal and steel, was just going a bit too fast for the French—a feeling that undercuts some of the attempts made to place French opposition to European integration in the 1960s on the shoulders of General de Gaulle alone. French caution and reservations have a far longer history than that, and, in their context, they are the counterpart to British reservations.

This point about French rejection of the EDC is borne out in a number of ways, not least the French acceptance of West German rearmament in principle as early as 1950. For another thing, the next time the six nations returned to their search for integration, they concentrated on far less ambitious projects, in so far as these projects involved national merging of sovereignty —namely the Treaties of Rome providing for customs union, economic union, and peacetime development of nuclear power. And the six partners in these ventures proceeded to develop their new communities one careful step at a time. But even more important were the immediate steps taken in the area of security. Only a few short weeks after the EDC treaty was rejected by the French National Assembly, the five Western Union countries agreed to broaden their organization to include West Germany and Italy, and took steps to provide for the raising of German forces. In the process, the Germans were subjected to even fewer controls in their armed forces—they were to have complete national divisions, although still no independent General Staff—and the French agreed to arrangements under which they had even less ability to dominate the use of these West German forces than they would have had under the EDC.

Significantly, the WEU agreements were proposed by the British—who also wished to stand aloof from integration in Europe, even more than did the French. Yet the British Government recognized that the American desire for German troops had to be met. Indeed, Mr Dulles had spoken of an 'agonizing reappraisal' if these demands were not met, and Britain was able, with little risk to her own independence of Europe, to satisfy this demand and gain some credit for resolving an impending crisis. Britain also pledged to keep four divisions (the British Army of the Rhine) and a tactical air force on the Continent, in theory until 1998, and would not withdraw them except with the permission of a majority of WEU powers in the event of 'an acute overseas emergency'. This was an effort to pacify European opinion about German rearmament. Yet the British began withdrawing these forces almost immediately, partly because of the Suez Crisis and financial pressures, and partly because the potential threat from West German troops seemed increasingly remote as the West Germans showed a marked and continuing reluctance to regain an army.

By this device—WEU—West German forces were brought into the structure of Western defence, and West Germany was brought into NATO. It did have to accept some inhibitions— such as the famous one against the manufacture of atomic, biological, and chemical weapons 'in its territory', but for all intents and purposes the West Germans became full allies, and Dr Adenauer had achieved his objective of making Germany respectable again.

The problem for European security lay in the impact that the entry of West Germany into WEU and NATO had on the Soviet Union. For these steps finally formalized the process of West Germany's increasing integration into a concept of Western defence, and formalized the division of that country into two parts.

Indeed, the Russian response was apparent almost immediately. From then on, the Russians dropped all pretence of flexibility on the issue of the division or reunification of Germany, and adopted a hard and consistent line of confrontation. There would be no new offers by the Russians to 'join NATO'; and no new approaches to resolve Germany's division through negotiation. Germany was finally divided in the sense that really counted—i.e. from the standpoint of whether a diplomatic effort were feasible in order to change that position. Whatever the prospects had been before, they were now dead. Until the logic of military confrontation worked itself out, there could be no real effort on either side to explore the possibilities of establishing security in Europe on any other basis than the simple formulation of two armed camps poised and ready to defend themselves against one another.

It is possible to argue that this integration of West Germany into NATO was one of the factors that led to the series of crises over the status of West Berlin between 1958 and 1961. These crises were, at least in part, an effort by Khruschev to clarify the position of the two Germanies—in other words, to create a basis of understanding that the existence of two Germanies had to be accepted as the start of any diplomatic process to change the pattern of confrontation in Europe. It is true that he wanted this clarification to take place at the expense of West Berlin's ties with West Germany, but at least there seemed here to be an effort to find a basis—of which recognition of East Germany by the West was the most important element—on which the anomalous position of a Germany not 'officially' divided would not continue to dominate the perspectives of the major powers on European security and, therefore, would no longer be a barrier to strengthening, preserving, and extending this security on the understanding that Germany *was* divided.

In so far as this is an accurate assessment of Soviet motivations, it illustrates the complications that were introduced into the process of achieving stability in Europe—both a political goal and a security interest—by West Germany's formal entry into NATO. The problem lay with what might be called the 'logic' of the West's having West Germany in NATO, while not at the same time recognizing East Germany—although in the context of NATO politics, this was done for understandable reasons, in view of the West Germans' desire for reunification. But now that the issue of Germany's division had become part of the formal structure of military confrontation, as opposed merely to being an outstanding political problem, then the working out of the logic of that confrontation came to include the need for mutual acceptance of a political and strategic *status quo* that entailed the formal division of Germany. And only with a broadening of this acceptance to include tacitly at least America and Russia did *détente* begin in Europe.

Within months of West Germany's entry into NATO, the Soviet Union constituted a military pact of its own in the East by a treaty signed in Warsaw on May 14, 1955. As discussed in Chapter 3, Russia and its seven satellites in Eastern Europe were brought together for the first time in a joint military venture. Previously—and, indeed, for at least the six years following, after which the Pact began to hold joint military exercises—the military relations between the Soviet Union and each of its seven satellite 'Allies' were conducted on a bilateral basis that formed the pattern of security in the Eastern *bloc*. But after the entry of West Germany into NATO, the Russians suddenly stood to gain some benefits from a formal military organization in direct confrontation with NATO.

To begin with, there was no longer any need for the Russians to maintain the fiction that Eastern *bloc* relations were less formalized than those of the West. In the apparent Russian view, there would be no diplomatic movement anyway, and therefore no worry about future difficulties of dismantling formal institutions, which would tend to focus attention along clear and rigid lines. Second, a formal organization might at least give an appearance of a more formidable opposition to

NATO—particularly a NATO containing West Germany—than mere bilateral defence pacts on their own. But most important, the entry of West Germany into NATO had given the Russians something they had very much needed: a convincing rationale for keeping the Eastern European countries wedded to the Soviet concept of security in Europe. Indeed, as early as the proposals for Western Union in 1948, the Russians had reacted by calling this a ruse to permit the establishment of an independent West German state. In 1955, the threat posed by the United States to Eastern Europe might have seemed remote; but the threat of West Germany—always a major concern of those states that had suffered most in the Second World War—was very near indeed. With West Germany now directly integrated into NATO, a greater rationale existed in Eastern *bloc* countries for making an active military effort and the possibility arose that a multilateral alliance would permit these countries to reinforce one another's perceptions of this threat. They would thus bind themselves even more closely to the Soviet view of West Germany and European security than they would do with only the simple bilateral relations with the Soviet Union and with one another.

But, as discussed in Chapter 3, it was not until after 1961—with the break-up of the Sino-Soviet Alliance, the defection of Albania to the Chinese camp, the arms build-up by the United States, the worries culminating in the building of the Berlin Wall, and the arms reductions at the beginning of the 1960s in Russia—that the Russians began to rely in a serious way on the Warsaw Pact. And through this there emerged—with joint manoeuvres, and even some Eastern European (mostly Roumanian) discontent with Russian domination of the military organs—a greater correspondence between the Warsaw Pact and NATO than there had been before.

But the significant point is that a simple view of these two security organizations as being even remotely comparable in their relations and functions does not do justice to the complexity of the reality of events in Europe. In short, the working out of a logic of military confrontation has depended far less upon development of relations between NATO and the Warsaw Pact, than upon the development of the relations between America and her NATO Allies on the one hand and, on the other hand, upon the Soviet Union's much more predominant strategic and political influence over her own Allies, particularly after the formal creation and later elaboration of a military pact in the East as part, initially, of Russia's own attitudes towards the 'German problem'.

Thus relations between East and West were made even more concrete and static by the entry of West Germany into NATO, and by the resulting inauguration of the Warsaw Pact. But there have been other ways in which the development of the security institutions—particularly NATO—have affected patterns of influence and confrontation.

To begin with, there has been the question of whether NATO could serve as the focus for any kind of Atlantic relations— or even European ones—that would go beyond the scope of purely military affairs. It has already been argued (Chapter 3) that the fundamental common interests of the Allies over the years can be reduced to two: namely, to preserve whatever level of defence might from time to time be thought necessary, and to keep the Americans committed to European security— particularly to preserve their nuclear guarantee.

This may seem a rather narrow definition—or even one that is unkind, in view of the tremendous efforts made to preserve Alliance unity and that ineffable substance 'cohesion'. But it is still largely true, as will be shown by a closer look at efforts over the years to broaden the scope of NATO. Indeed, 'cohesion' within the Alliance has only been possible when there has been a high degree of mutual appreciation of at least some military threat from the Russians and agreement as to its potential target. In other words, there has had to be agreement to keep the focus of the Alliance at its most narrow.

But having in mind questions of European integration and Atlantic relations, the framers of the North Atlantic treaty did include an article that dealt (in the most general and vague terms) with problems of political understanding and—more precisely—economic relations. This was Article 2, which provided, in part, that member states should 'seek to eliminate conflict in their international economic relations and will encourage economic collaboration between any or all of them'. (See Appendix II.) And ever since, there has been a question whether anything concrete could be made of these provisions. Nothing of substance ever has been, however, partly because the very size of the NATO organization has prevented the definition of sufficient common interest to make it the focus of economic or other co-operative ventures. Instead, these have been centred on the European Economic Community, the European Free Trade Association, the General Agreement on Tariffs and Trade (with a membership even wider than NATO's, but dealing with very specific problems) or the Group of Ten. The Council of Europe, on the other hand, with its broader focus but more limited mandate, has been a dismal failure at achieving anything at all significant: even it seems to include too many nations with diverging political and economic interests.

This is not to say that there have not been efforts over the years to turn NATO into something more than a mutual security pact. Indeed, there has been a succession of trials— and failures—right up to the 20th anniversary of the organization. The most important of these efforts began in 1956, with the report of a special committee of the North Atlantic Council, composed of Sr Marino from Italy, Mr Lange from Norway, and Mr Pearson from Canada (the 'three wise men'—NATO's second set, the first having put together the Lisbon Force Goals in 1951–52). They proposed a broadening of the Alliance to include increased co-operation in economic, scientific, political and cultural affairs. In particular, there were to be greater efforts on the part of the Allies to settle their differences inside the NATO context instead of outside it.

It is significant that the Committee of Three and its sponsors reflected the opinion largely of the smaller powers of NATO, which saw in the new arrangements for consultation a chance to dilute some of the preponderant influence of the larger powers, meaning in particular that of the United States. And because of the idealistic nature of the proposals, the major powers concurred in their adoption.

The new purposes even met with some success. For example, in the Cyprus crisis of 1958, in which three NATO Allies were involved (Britain, Greece and Turkey), the good offices of NATO did play some part in a resolution of the crisis on a more-or-less amicable basis. Significantly, in the Cyprus crisis of 1964–65, after this NATO consultative process had been allowed to decay, NATO's influence in settling the dispute was much less marked. And, again in 1958, the NATO forum helped to resolve a dispute between Britain and Iceland over fishing rights.

But it was still difficult for any of the major allies—or, for that matter, for many of the minor allies, whether or not they had outside interests (as in early disputes on residual colonial problems)—to see NATO as a forum for resolving disputes that went beyond the limited liabilities imposed by the North Atlantic Treaty. In particular, as will be developed below, NATO proved woefully inadequate—almost by common consent—in dealing with problems that arose outside the NATO treaty area itself.

Yet there still was some limited effort towards conducting political consultations within a NATO context on matters that could prove contentious among various Allies. In time, even that process broke down, largely because of the new attitude towards NATO adopted by the Kennedy Administration which came to power in 1961. It was not so much a *new* attitude; rather, it was perhaps a more aggressive (i.e. less diplomatic) assertion of the potential of American influence that had always been present. Fundamentally, the idea of submitting American problems located outside the treaty area (e.g. Vietnam) to the Council did not appeal to the new Administration, and the procedures for consultation on a regular basis adopted in 1956 were quietly allowed to fall into disuse. In later years, there have been some joint efforts at consulting—or, rather, informing—Allies, but these never recaptured the tenuous yet tangible quality of Allied political consultations during the years 1956–1961, which by no coincidence also happened to be the years that General Lauris Norstad was in command at Supreme Headquarters, Allied Powers Europe.

Thus ended the grand experiment with Article 2, although ten years after the report of the Committee of Three, there were still celebrations in NATO about its forward-looking and idealistic character.

This experiment was significant, if only because it illustrated the very narrow basis of common interest on which the NATO Alliance has been based. It also presaged the difficulties that would be encountered if ever the Alliance were to be used as a forum for discussing ways of recasting political confrontation in Europe—indeed, of finding any way of changing the existing pattern of confrontation. Each member nation, in fact, has had certain interests which it prefers to pursue on its own, or at least on a strictly bilateral basis with one or another Ally. The patina of Alliance unity ('cohesion') has rarely been permitted to obscure the pursuit of these interests.

From time to time, there has even been some measure of resentment at efforts by Allies to use the Alliance for what others might term extraneous purposes. Some American efforts to stimulate greater European political integration (as through the Multilateral Force) met with resistance almost as much because of the attempt to channel much of the effort through NATO as for the nature of the pressure itself.

From the point of view of overall European security, this failure of the NATO Allies may have had salutary benefits (if 'failure' is an appropriate word to describe a process that has been so little grounded in practical politics). After all, despite the increased difficulties that would be posed by Allied consultations on problems of change in patterns of European confrontation, the lack of a broad base for the Alliance has also meant that such change across the East-West division has remained a greater possibility than might otherwise have been the case. Lacking certain elements of greater political or economic integration NATO, as a forum, would have less to dismantle if ever the prospect arose of ending the military confrontation and bridging the gap, politically or economically, between East and West Europe.

Throughout all these years, there has been a basic formula for observing what has often been called the 'cohesion' of the Alliance—in effect, the willingness of the Allies to accommodate to one another on matters that have not pertained directly to the most important matters of mutual security. Simply, as mentioned earlier, when there has appeared to be a high degree of Soviet threat, there has been a greater sense of cohesion—i.e. of willingness to work together; and when that threat has diminished, so has cohesion. But this has not been entirely a matter of laziness in the face of a reduced threat. For as suggested above, an increase in cohesion within the Alliance would also mean a more formalized division of the Continent, and fewer prospects for change of a political, economic, or other nature. Therefore, the appearance of 'threat' from the Russians—in whatever form—has been not so much a signal that defences have had to be increased, as it has been that the prospects for change have once more receded. And it is in this context—and in this one alone—that the Russian invasion of Czechoslovakia in 1968 may be said to represent an increased Soviet 'threat' to European security.

This also helps to explain why, during times of tension, American requests for increased troop levels in Europe have so often been received on the Continent with such bad grace. It has been, of course, partly a matter of Europeans' worrying about the credibility of the American nuclear guarantee if conventional forces were to be increased (see Chapter 4). But it has also been a matter that cohesion has been regarded merely as the political alternative to accommodating US demands for increased troop levels, at times when hopes for change have been proving unrealistic. This was what happened in the autumn of 1968, when the Soviet invasion of Czechoslovakia signalled the postponement of prospects for change in Europe, and therefore helped to increase the political cohesion of the Alliance: not so much because there was any belief in an increased military threat to Western Europe (even the force increases were really only of diplomatic significance in indicating Western displeasure), as there was an awareness of the need to take *political* steps to make *détente* in Europe possible once again. If a warning to the Russians were required, in order to establish, once again, the conditions for *détente* (and later for change), then so be it: the Russians would be shown—through increased cohesion in the West—that the price they had to pay for *détente* with the West was restraint in the East.

But at least the Allies at times have agreed to make an effort to find some means of co-ordinating opinion. The most important of these efforts was undertaken officially through a study commissioned for the North Atlantic Council in 1967 (the 'Harmel Report'), and presented to the Council at the end of that year. Despite the fanfare with which it was launched, the Harmel Report (Appendix 7) once again demonstrated the almost impossible nature of the task of co-ordinating Alliance policy for the future. Indeed, it can be argued that it would have been better not to advertise the difficulties obviously facing the Alliance as it tried to cope with the future. What was the purpose, after all, of worrying about the cohesion of the Alliance—and the integrity, for political purposes, of Allied Command Europe—if one were going to proclaim that the Allies could not really find ways to reconcile their differences in exploiting the *détente*, or in going beyond this to *entente* or even to engagement?

There were platitudes in the report, of course, but little that was concrete. All that *was* concrete was still to be found in policies pursued by individual nations, such as the United States, which has been searching simultaneously for a way to deal with a Soviet-American *détente*, its pledges to West Germany about German reunification, and the perennial problems of trying to hold the Western Alliance together. In fact, the Americans have so far been unable to reconcile these different objectives, and their dilemma has become even more apparent since the Czech invasion (see Chapter 6).

But it has been the French, at least under President de Gaulle, who have seen most clearly the dangers in cohesion pursued for its own sake, so long as the Alliance is unable to define criteria for turning *détente* into something more positive. It is not that criteria cannot be discovered—that proposition has yet to be proved—but that they have eluded Alliance statesmen. For the French under de Gaulle, therefore, the alternative was relatively simple—to prepare for the exploitation of *détente* on their own. And so they did, with General de Gaulle's series of *démarches* to the Alliance in 1966. By dropping the pretence that cohesion in the Alliance had any value outside a situation of real threat, General de Gaulle appeared to believe that he could gain greater flexibility in dealing with the Russians.

In the event, the 'realities' of American predominance in Western Europe led this policy to misfire (though not entirely to fail), as it became clear that France could obtain nothing in the direction of change in European confrontation without American acquiescence. But at least the French were looking in that direction, and succeeded in hastening the search among the rest of the Western Allies for ways to change the patterns of confrontation in Europe.

With the Russian invasion of Czechoslovakia, the French made some changes in their position—not by rejoining the integrated military structure of NATO, but rather by edging diplomatically closer to their Allies. As with the Allied reaction, itself, the new French position can be seen as an effort to demonstrate to the Russians that the pursuit of *détente* requires Russian restraint in Eastern Europe—as well as a toleration of change in the Eastern *bloc* that, in itself, does not affect Russian security in any real sense—if *détente* is to be mutually beneficial.

At the same time, the French began to co-operate with the Allies in their surveillance of Russian naval activities in the Mediterranean.

But if the problem of getting agreement among the 15 Allies —or even a portion of them—has proved difficult in matters directly relating to Europe (such as the best manner for bringing about a change in the pattern of European confrontation), it has proved almost impossible where questions outside the NATO treaty area have been concerned.

There has been no lack of trying. From the beginning of the Alliance, one Ally or another has tried to use the Alliance for its own national purposes outside the carefully delimited geographical limits of the Alliance's guarantees. In the first place, the question of the scope of the treaty's purview—did it, even in a philosophical sense, embrace all the Western interests in the world?—entered into the process of burden-sharing. What element of a nation's defence expenditures could be included? Just those spent directly in the defence of Europe, or all of them, wherever spent?

Throughout most of NATO's history, this problem has been settled by a crude process of bargaining, and by competition (particularly among European powers) to see which country could default the most on its commitments without endangering the Alliance structure. But some issues have been brought into the open. For one thing, each of the Allies with colonial possessions when the Treaty was signed—the Netherlands, Britain, France, Portugal, Belgium—claimed special dispensation for the forces required to maintain overseas garrisons. And, of course, the United States indirectly claimed such dispensation every time the general standard of percentage of gross national product spent on defence was introduced as a criterion for assessing 'fair shares'. Perhaps it has been appropriate that the United States, on balance over the whole period, has borne the brunt of NATO financing throughout the world, by this standard of percentage invested of total GNP. After all, the United States has clearly received the greatest share of influence and security for its investments in other parts of the world. Of course, this begs the question—who benefits most? if at all —in the European context from military efforts outside the treaty area. But it does, at least, illustrate the problem of relating American global involvements—and the question of their relevance to strictly European security—with the more limited ones of even the most widely involved European ally, at least after the global involvements of Britain and France fell behind those of the United States.

The problem of the role to be played by NATO in areas outside the treaty area has had even more direct relevance to the development of Alliance relations. There have been specific conflicts and problems that have led various Allies to ask for outside aid. There have been instances in which colonial powers demanded the support of their Allies—culminating in the fulminations of Prime Minister Salazar in 1966 about the failure of NATO to give adequate support to Portuguese colonial policies in Angola and Mozambique. There was, of course, the extraordinary row within NATO over the Suez war, when the Americans thwarted the efforts of the British and French. At one time the French wanted NATO's support for their policies in Algeria; at others the Americans have tried to keep Britain involved east of Suez; and there has been the long-standing American effort to link NATO with the war in Vietnam. Ironically, it was the French who first tried to get support from the Allies in Southeast Asia; and they received certain verbal assurances in the form of resolutions. But when the Americans tried it, they got even less, time after time, no matter how hard their spokesmen tried to present that war as an extension of the defence of Western Europe.

Throughout the history of NATO, therefore, these efforts to involve the Alliance elsewhere in the world have met with almost total failure. This was so largely for the basic reason of narrow common interests: it was difficult enough to get 15 nations to agree at any one time on the nature of the Soviet threat in Europe (if there ever was agreement); it was infinitely more difficult to get any one of the Allies, except where bilateral commitments were concerned, to agree to help another Ally in need outside that area.

This remained true even when in 1958 the French tried to restructure the Alliance—and all commitments of the major Western powers. At that time the Americans—not without considerable justification—merely noted that 'it was simply not possible to establish an organic directorate either over NATO or the rest of the world'. On the other hand, this event demonstrated a central problem that has plagued NATO, and would certainly plague any larger organization or broader-based Alliance: namely, the tremendous difficulties of establishing patterns of influence among different countries, where the partial merging of sovereignties—even in so limited a venture as NATO—comes up against divergences of political interest. In the NATO context, these divergences of political interest would be more inhibiting as they became more profound and deviated further from the limited goal of a common defence against a common and palpable threat.

There was yet another objective of the Harmel Report in 1967—and another of its conspicuous failures: the attempt to gain some common basis for co-ordinating the activities of individual NATO nations in the outside world. But there simply was no basis for working together where there was no common threat to perceived interests, nor much chance of finding an effective mechanism for the adequate sharing of influence— that most evanescent, yet most troublesome, of all the elements of the NATO Alliance.

Yet this situation was not necessarily to be regretted when seen from the standpoint of any possibility of extending the NATO-Warsaw Pact pattern of military confrontation beyond the confines of Europe. By keeping the scope of NATO limited to Europe, the Allies reduced the chance of spreading the context of confrontation to other areas of the world. During the 1950s, to be sure, the nature of the US-Soviet relationship came to mean that virtually any new area in which one super-power found itself involved almost surely attracted the other, as well. The confrontation was regarded as global (at least by Dulles and his ilk) and in a sense became indivisible.

It was difficult enough, in terms of keeping separate various spheres of possible confrontation, to have 15 nations belonging to NATO; it would have been even more difficult if the NATO Alliance had become a seamless web stretching throughout the range of Western interests. How then could there have been accommodation between East and West anywhere, without the most profound consequences for the structure of the overall 'super' Alliance, and for the problem of cohesion?

This question has direct significance when seen in relationship to other American-sponsored or supported security alliances conceived during the early 1950s, from the Central Treaty Organization (CENTO—an outgrowth of the Baghdad Pact), to the ANZUS Treaty and the South-east Asia Treaty Organization (SEATO). The more nations there were with their security bound up within the same institutionalized context of confrontation, the more difficult it would be to see that context transformed into a phase of accommodation. There could even be added impediments placed in the way of settling outstanding political problems whose settlement might be of compelling interest to nations at one end of an Alliance, but be of relatively little concern to those at the other. After all, what real interest have the West Germans had—much less the Danes—in possible conflicts of interest between the Russians and the Turks? Beyond the need to preserve some semblance of cohesion, almost for its own sake, there must be very little value to be gained from concern with Turkey by a Government in Bonn or Copenhagen that is contemplating the prospects for pursuing the position and role of *détente* across the Central Front of Europe itself.

CENTO is particularly instructive in this regard—i.e. in considering the political functions that can be performed by an alliance beyond the simple guarantees of security, however broadly defined, that are implicit in its basic agreement.

CENTO is particularly worth a brief comparison since, in one case in the local area—namely Turkey—there has been overlapping membership with NATO.

Yet there have rarely been any ideas put forward for transforming CENTO into an institution to further political integration among its three local members—Turkey, Iran, and Pakistan: three states which have seldom even been able to agree on the nature or even the existence of any Soviet 'threat' to their interests. In the case of Pakistan, in particular, the CENTO Alliance, at least in recent years, has been seen to be of almost no 'security' value at all, since United States support for CENTO (through a series of bilateral agreements) is specifically limited to threats emanating from communist sources, and provides no support at all to Pakistan in its dispute with India over Kashmir—a far more real issue of security for the Government in Rawalpindi.

Indeed, the significance that CENTO has retained—since the beginning of a process of resolving conflicts with the Soviet Union largely over local issues that antedate the Soviet-American competition in Europe—has been in the field of economics. But even this has not been conceived, as in Western Europe, as a functional approach to integration; instead it is a limited effort to approach common economic problems of developing nations through joint efforts supported by Britain, the only outside member of CENTO, and by the United States, the more or less 'affiliated' partner. The Regional Co-operation for Development[1] provides what impetus there remains to hold CENTO together; yet this has neither stimulated American or other pressures for converting this into functional integration, nor especially aroused American anxieties about future security requirements in this area along the southern borders of the Soviet Union—security requirements that were seen to be of such importance in the late 1940s, during the formulation of the Truman Doctrine. Even increasing contact by each of the three

[1] Set up by Iran, Pakistan, and Turkey in 1964 and deliberately kept by them *outside* the framework in CENTO.

local CENTO Powers with the Soviet Union has not, as yet at least, caused the US undue alarm, even though in the case of Iran this has led to trade with the Soviet Union involving the supply by the Russians of as much as $110 million worth of certain types of armaments.

The different attitudes shown by the Western partners of CENTO to developments in that region, in contrast to the US attitude towards the integrity of the NATO Alliance, are not so much the result of a greater sense of stability in the CENTO region, *vis-à-vis* the Soviet Union. In fact, there is certainly a good deal less 'security' there, and without the same kinds of political and strategic understandings between the two super-powers that obtain across the Central Front of Europe. Nor can the less vital importance of the CENTO region entirely explain this difference in attitude concerning the effective collapse of CENTO as a collective pact for security, on the one hand, and the political anxieties for the future expressed—and given a kind of concrete form in the very commissioning of a Harmel Report on the 'Future Tasks of the Alliance'—in the case of NATO.

The answer to this apparent puzzle lies more in the non-military functions being served by the two Alliances. In the case of CENTO, little is expected by the United States of the local powers—for example, they have not been subjected to the same concerted and public pressures to support US policy in Vietnam—and they, in turn, expect little from the United States beyond a measure of economic assistance and a residual commitment against an undefined and almost unspoken possible 'threat' to their political interests that could re-emerge from the Soviet Union. There is a partial exception to this pattern in the case of Turkey. But the significant point here is that Turkey has chosen to express its security anxieties within the context of NATO, not that of CENTO. It is true that in NATO there has been generated a greater sense of American commitment, but for Turkey's purposes this is a commitment that derives at least in part from the high value placed by the Americans, in particular, on the question of alliance cohesion. And this is to say nothing of the value that this cohesion has acquired as an end in itself within the NATO Alliance, almost without reference to any functional uses to which cohesion may be put.

Turkey, therefore, is more likely to achieve its security objectives—largely taking the form of an American guarantee—within the scope of the NATO Alliance than through CENTO or even on a bilateral basis—i.e. it has succeeded in posing as a 'European' power. And the seriousness with which NATO councils study Turkish claims for 'nuclear land mines', for example, seems to indicate at least that this approach has merit for the Turks, put in terms of the integrity of the entire NATO Alliance. And the merit of this approach has also been demonstrated in the creation of the ACE (Allied Command Europe) Mobile Force, a small military force designed at least in part with Turkey in mind, and in general almost entirely as a political device to promote the elusive political 'cohesion', especially in the outlying areas of the Alliance.

But the comparison between CENTO and NATO, within the context of the non-military uses of an Alliance, can be taken even further. As argued above, the process of change in patterns of confrontation is vitally affected by the number of nations with interests in the outcome of this process.

The more nations involved, the more difficult it will prove to use, say, NATO, as an effective instrument for settling on common future political objectives virtually anywhere within the compass of the North Atlantic Treaty area, *vis-à-vis* Soviet political and security interests as defined in Moscow. Within CENTO, no such process is envisaged: there is, for a start, no outstanding problem of a divided Germany, nor any legacy of a former dominant power whose reunification is still widely seen in terms of the stereotypes of 1939, at a time when today's two super-powers remained aloof from European security problems.

And, again, there is in the CENTO Alliance no significant institutional framework, including a peace-time military command structure and actual forces under Allied command. Hence, there is not the same sense of a military 'logic of confrontation' that has had to be worked through between the United States and the Soviet Union in the CENTO region as there has been in central Europe itself. Nor is there any elaborate apparatus that must be dismantled, and seen to be dismantled, as the Americans and Russians pursue a limited form of political accommodation in the CENTO region that fully exploits the political ambiguities that exist, and apparently has been judged by both sides to be worth more than the 'certainties' that derive from a frozen and sterile military confrontation.

But more important, perhaps, is again the whole question of the role played by NATO over the years for bargaining out the relationship between the United States and its Western European Allies—a process (or rather an interlocking series of processes) that the United States has never really channelled to Turkey, Iran, and Pakistan through the CENTO organization as such. And within NATO this is a process of bargaining out a relationship that is becoming of critical importance where the pursuit of *détente* either by the United States directly with the Soviet Union for their common interest (on such matters as arms control), or perhaps even by Europeans, has become the dominant focus and concern of the NATO Alliance and of relative American and Western European interests.

As a result, the end of the old context of military confrontation as between NATO and the Warsaw Pact—the working out of the logic—argues strongly that the process of bargaining within the West on matters of *détente*, and particularly in reconciling those divergent American and Western European interests that have been made quite evident since the Soviet invasion of Czechoslovakia, be limited to as few nations as possible.

Indeed, the process of changing the patterns of confrontation in Europe, as opposed to maintaining the strength of those patterns, is more likely to succeed where issues can be isolated within contexts where there can be mutual agreement by both East and West. This is why recent increases in Soviet fleet deployments in the Mediterranean, beginning about 1964, have really been so disturbing to NATO: they could appear to pose new 'threats' of a limited nature to more outlying areas of the Alliance, as well as to Italy, a nation which has come to be seen as part of the Central Front, however unjustified this may be in terms of genuine European security problems. And these new 'threats' come at a time when, followed by an appeal for Alliance 'cohesion', progress towards solving problems across the Central Front with the nations of the Warsaw Pact could well be retarded.

It is arguable that a new context should be considered for structuring American guarantees to the Eastern Mediterranean countries in NATO, at least the guarantees to Turkey if not also to Greece, because of the greater significance of neighbouring Yugoslavia to the West in terms of the prospects for *détente* in Central Europe following the invasion of Czechoslovakia. The Balkan Pact (Treaty of Ankara), concluded between Greece, Turkey and Yugoslavia in 1953, and developed into a full defensive alliance in 1954, might provide such a focus for US participation in the Eastern Mediterranean that would leave the rest of Western Europe free for recasting the context of confrontation with the Warsaw Pact. This would depend, of course, on both Russian and Yugoslav attitudes towards something of a lessening of the ambiguities surrounding the position of Yugoslavia. Alternatively, there could be bilateral guarantees to Greece and Turkey—guarantees that would enable the United States to bring its commitments to these countries more properly into line with a structure that is capable of taking care of them without encountering the stifling problems of cohesion within the NATO Alliance.

These are really matters of *détente* and properly belong in a discussion of that particular subject. But there is at least one other matter that cannot be ignored in a discussion of the non-military functions of the NATO Alliance, and that is the extent to which the very structuring of an Alliance and of East-West confrontation has driven underground, so to speak, some of the residual political problems that exist in a muted form within

Europe, however Europe is defined—i.e. problems and conflicts that would tend to re-emerge if there were ever a resolution of the central conflict dividing the Continent. This concept may apply especially to traditional enmities among nations of southeast Europe, whether Greek-Turkish disputes that have not been entirely submerged by the overriding need for 'cohesion' as it has been expressed within the context of NATO, or disputes among Balkan countries within or adjoining the Warsaw Pact. But there is also the more pressing problem of the relations between Germany—however structured—and its neighbours. The fundamental dictum of French policy on this issue since the Second World War—*rapprochement*—will be made no easier by the approach of real chances to change existing patterns of European confrontation. Indeed, this central problem of Germany will probably become more difficult to resolve—or at least will become of more immediate concern to all its neighbours who, again, will be operating perhaps with outdated stereotypes, if and when the issue of reunification becomes again one of central importance and discussion.

And introduction of this subject brings the discussion in the latter part of this chapter back to the basic question posed, and hardly answered, by the Harmel Report. That question remains whether NATO could be a forum for pursuing *détente*, and for carrying it beyond to *entente* and engagement.

Unfortunately, there is little in NATO's history to justify such a hope. It is not just the poor record of consultation—partly because of the great disparity in power among the Allies and the failure of American efforts to create a politically-unified 'equal' in Europe for the 'Atlantic Partnership'. There are also what appear to be the radically different political interests of the several Allies in a world in which they are not confronted with a simplistic and one-dimensional Soviet military threat across central Europe. Indeed, the failure of the Harmel Report to produce anything more than promises to try finding answers, further indicates that it is nearly impossible to find in NATO an adequate forum for handling these problems—or to handle them in joint diplomatic efforts by NATO and the Warsaw Pact. Of course, the Warsaw Pact may prove equally inadequate as a forum for consultation, if such a time is ever reached that the Soviet Union will consider changes in patterns of European confrontation that will be acceptable to East and West Europeans alike.

But there is still much that has to be said about the nature of *détente* in Europe, about its impact on the continuing problems of European security, and about the possible character of a new pattern of confrontation, even if there is no clear way of transforming the patterns of 1949–69 into those postulated for the future.

Chapter 6

The Development of *Détente*

The process commonly known as *détente* has had many sources, some of which have already been presented, but which are worth recapitulating. In the first place, there was the beginning of strategic stability as between the United States and the Soviet Union at the strategic nuclear level, when it became apparent in 1962–63 that both countries could each survive any attack by the other, and retaliate with devastating consequences. Second, there was a perception by both super-powers at the end of 1962 that the Cuban Missile Crisis had taken the world uncomfortably near the brink of nuclear war, over issues that were not politically worth such a threat to end the world. From then on, both the Americans and the Russians conducted their affairs with a great deal more caution than they had exercised before. And there were other factors, including the Sino-Soviet split and the spiralling costs of the arms race, which implied the need for greater inhibitions in the behaviour of the super-powers.

But within the context of Europe, as distinct from that solely of the super-powers, the most important factor making for *détente* was the acceptance both in East and West that there was no longer much to be gained, and considerable risks to be run, in attempting to alter the pattern of confrontation to the advantage of one side or the other.

This view had been shared by most Europeans, in both NATO and the Warsaw Pact, for many years. But the climate of acceptance necessary for this to become a real relaxation of tensions depended upon the realization on the part of the super-powers that their own best interests lay in an end to the recurring crises, such as those over Berlin, that had prevented the *status quo* from being permanently formalized and thereby made a firm basis for negotiation.

But despite a long-standing realization throughout the Continent that European security depended on an acceptance of at least the strategic division of Europe, there remained in 1962 the problem of Germany—a problem defined both by latent fears of reunification on the part of all of Germany's neighbours (fears long exploited by the Soviet Union)—and by the West Germans' continual insistence that reunification was a major objective of their policy. Indeed, for the next few years after 1962 and the beginning of *détente*, the major unsettled question in the Western Alliance related to the extent to which this *détente* could be permitted to proceed without some understanding on the potential future of Germany. This question lay behind much of the debate about 'nuclear sharing' and the Multilateral Force: that is, would the interests of all the Western Allies in exploiting the possibilities of *détente* coincide, or would there be major strains in the Alliance as the result of diverging interests? This study has already considered some of the problems—intrinsic to any alliance that tries to change the basis on which it has been organized. But the question of differing perspectives during the early stages of *détente* went even beyond this. In the years following the Cuban Missile Crisis—a convenient watershed to date the onset of at least widespread perceptions of *détente*—considerable diplomatic activity within NATO was centred on this one question: how could the West Germans best be kept in step with the process of *détente*, without having to be granted the assurance that every step in *détente* would be subject to their veto? This was largely an American problem, but not exclusively so. For in the period 1962–68, the general interest of West Europeans in *détente* roughly coincided with that of the Americans: the former saw that *détente* could help to bring about a change in the pattern of confrontation in Europe, and was already showing signs of furthering East-West contacts, including some liberalization of communist régimes in the East; and the latter came to see the utmost benefit in turning away from the fears, tensions and sheer economic costs of an uncontrolled arms race and a series of European crises with the Russians. The Russians, of course, also shared this interest and seemed—at least until the summer of 1968—to accept that the maintenance of *détente* also required them to permit some semblance of internal liberalization in the Eastern *bloc* countries.

But for West Germany—and, indeed, also for the German Democratic Republic, a state still lacking the full panoply of legitimacy conferred on the Bonn Government—there was not the same correspondence of view with that of other West European states and the super-powers. There were, indeed, acute fears in West Germany that either the United States or some grouping of West European states would be willing to sacrifice, or at least to postpone, the interests of German reunification either for the sake of arms control, in the case of the United States, or for a form of reunification in Europe. General de Gaulle was quick to identify this problem, and did what he could both to reassure the West Germans and to gain diplomatic leverage *vis-à-vis* London and Washington by seeming to help Bonn to secure its overriding objective. He worked to conclude a Paris-Bonn Axis, the culmination of which was the Franco-German Treaty of 1963. For most of the following years, however, this treaty has had little effect except to symbolize one of the goals of the original European Coal and Steel Community—namely, to make war between France and Germany impossible and to herald the end of a 90-year old quarrel; but with a clear recognition that France was the dominant power in the partnership.

The West Germans were still concerned about *American* intentions. After all, only the Americans (in conjunction with the Russians) could really sanction a change in the status of the division of Europe and of Germany. Whatever the French could attempt with regard to rapprochement with Bonn, coupled with diplomatic efforts in Moscow, could not change this fundamental and continuing US role as the dominant power in

Western Europe, as even the Russians with rare lapses have acknowledged—and, indeed, have often insisted upon.

Yet as the process of *détente* seemed to gain momentum—at least as far as US-Soviet relations were concerned—there began to be a shift in emphasis in West German policy. There was, to begin with, a gradual change of the old Adenauer policy of playing 'good Germans' in the West—a change that began under Chancellor Erhard, but was accelerated under Dr Kiesinger, who was even better placed to see the movement in recent years towards a divergence between American and European interests in the process of *détente*.

But the basic shift in the emphasis of West German interests towards connections with France (including West Germany's ready acceptance of the continued stationing of French forces in the Federal Republic, almost regardless of the status of these forces) was reinforced by another event—namely, a major re-definition of American policy towards Europe and the process of *détente* that was made by President Johnson in October 1966. The essence of this redefinition of policy represented only a reversal of priorities: no longer, Mr Johnson implied, would German reunification be seen as an event to take place on its own, nor would it remain a goal to be seen in isolation. Rather, it was to be seen as part of a process of change throughout Europe, in which it might be necessary to find conditions for ending the artificial division of Europe before approaches could be made to settling the more parochial German problem.

This redefinition of American policy was undoubtedly the most forward-looking and realistic assessment of the actual conditions required for change in patterns of European confrontation. And it did not lead to a radical realignment of forces in the Alliance, with the Continental Allies grouped on the one hand, and *'les Anglo-Saxons'* on the other. But it did create the potential for disagreement if a divergence of opinion or interest should occur between the Americans and the others about the worth of a continuing *détente* with the Russians. After all, here were the Americans once again prescribing political strategies for Western Europe, however much the 'Germany second' approach might have appealed to other West Europeans. But even more, this re-definition of the US attitude towards *détente* also implied an American desire to proceed with purely bilateral US-Soviet relations—a process that would coincide with Western European interests only so long as there were corresponding gains in terms of improved West European relations with the East. Yet in the context of the Johnson speech in 1966, only the West Germans seemed to be losing something by the course being taken by *détente*.

Then, with the Soviet invasion of Czechoslovakia in August 1968, there came the divergence of US interests and those of the West European states in general. Almost immediately, the identity vanished between the American interest in developing as wide an area of agreement with the Russians as possible, and the West European interest, no longer limited to the West Germans, to see that the benefits of increased contacts with the East applied to all the Allies. The prospects for the latter were rapidly disappearing. How could the West Europeans accept a *détente* while the Russians demonstrated that they were still willing to go to any lengths to reverse the liberalization movement in Czechoslovakia? Even worse, if such were possible, did the Russian invasion also end the prospect that there could be a gradual erosion of political barriers, within a context of strategic stability, which would eventually lead to a political reconstitution of the Continent that would be to everyone's benefit? To many West Europeans, the Russians did not appear to share the hopeful view that *détente* could apply to relations between Eastern European states and the outside world, and lead to increased autonomy in their internal development as well.

This widely-shared disillusionment in Western Europe stemmed at least in part from a faulty concept in the West about the conditions needed to bring about a change in the pattern of confrontation. As had been the case of Soviet-American relations before 1962, too much attention had been focused on the nature of the strategic environment in Europe, and not enough on the actual development of political relations among European states across the old East-West barrier. It was true that East-West relations on the political level had improved with almost startling ease, but there were grave errors of judgement in the West—for once, almost universally shared —about the limits to improving those political relations without carefully defining their significance within a context of Soviet interests. And this was a context that the Russians, themselves, could only construct.

After *détente* had been under way for some time, there developed in the West a concept that very considerable political changes would be possible, provided only that the new accepted strategic *status quo* in Europe were not threatened by either the Western Powers or by the Soviet Union. For some time, this proved true. As a result, the process of liberalization under Mr Dubček was contrasted with the almost totally different one which had been taking place in Roumania, a state which remained essentially Stalinist while challenging Soviet leadership within the Warsaw Pact. In the West, therefore, this Roumanian challenge had been regarded as posing the more fundamental challenge to Russia, because of the Western emphasis on Russia's security rather than on its political interests that went beyond security.

Thus the Soviet invasion of Czechoslovakia upset Western calculations about the extent to which strategic stability in Europe would alone automatically provide the basis for profound political changes. After all, the Dubček government had been scrupulous in reassuring the Russians that nothing being done in Czechoslovakia would jeopardize Soviet security interests. But, in retrospect, there has emerged some evidence for judging Soviet interests in terms that go beyond the simple strategic questions. After all, the 1948 coup in Prague did nothing to change the strategic *status quo* in Europe—even then, Czechoslovakia was almost universally considered to be within the Russian centre of activities for any strategic purpose. And in 1948 there had been astonishment almost equal to that of

1968 (at least in Britain and Western Europe) that the Russians should have brought about a *coup* in a country which already stood firmly on their side in the slowly coalescing strategic 'balance' in Europe.

In any event, after August 1968, it was apparent that the process of *détente* was, for the nations of Western Europe, a much more difficult task than had been presumed. It appeared that the Russians were going to insist on having a free hand on their side of the strategic frontier—that is, the Russians were to extend the tentatively accepted concept of a *strategic* 'sphere of influence', reaffirmed rather than invalidated by their invasion of Czechoslovakia, to encompass a *political* 'sphere of influence' with such far-reaching implications. Therefore, the West Europeans could expect little direct benefit from accepting the American definition of the need for a Western search for areas of accommodation with the Soviet Union. And, as far as West Germany in particular was concerned, the prospects of reunification seemed even more remote, whether it was to be achieved as a by-product of general changes in Europe, or through the success of a direct functional approach to East Germany that had been part of the Federal Republic's so-called *Ostpolitik*.

Significantly, though, the NATO countries rejected the notion that the Soviet invasion of Czechoslovakia should be countered by a major build-up of forces, as though there had been a real increase in the Russian threat—indeed, there was not even a general NATO alert during the invasion and the Russians took the most scrupulous care to inform Western Governments that they were not being threatened with invasion. The NATO countries decided that there should be some build-ups, but more as a means of indicating to the Russians that to continue their *détente* with the Americans—and Moscow called almost immediately for the start of arms control talks—would require a major change in the Russian attitude towards Czecho-slovakia and the two other 'apostate' powers, Roumania and Yugoslavia. In this process, the long-standing opponents within

NATO of the concept of 'political warning time' and of the distinction between Russian military capabilities and political intentions, helped to create the climate necessary for Russia to be made aware of the price of continuing *détente* with the United States. But nowhere in the Alliance was there a real scare about an increased 'threat' to NATO. Even in West Germany, the logic of the context of military confrontation had worked itself out—even there the 'mould' seemed to have been broken—and it was unlikely to be revived without some very concrete evidence of new Soviet aggressiveness: not aggressiveness against Russia's nominal Allies, nor even in peripheral areas of the world, including the Mediterranean, but against the NATO Central Front itself.

For a time, the American Government also seemed to accept this reasoning, on behalf of its NATO Allies, and ceased pressing for the arms control measures to which it had been so firmly committed a few months before. And it was only after the American election campaign, and President Nixon's early visit to Western Europe in February 1969, that the Americans felt able to reconcile their desire to begin arms limitation talks with the Russians with the anxieties of the West Europeans that the invasion of Czechoslovakia should in no way appear to be rewarded.

But, in the meantime, the NATO Allies took a formal step of their own. This took the form of a warning about the consequences of possible Soviet moves against countries which were unnamed, but certainly included Yugoslavia at the very least. This warning by NATO was widely seen within a context of what seemed to be a real threat to at least one Eastern European country—Roumania—but it was really concerned with something more basic than a Soviet threat to any particular state. Rather, it concerned the conditions under which it could fairly be said that the Russians were 'playing the game' of searching for a new pattern of European security arrangements. Put simply, there were few West Europeans who would place much value on any attempt to go beyond NATO, if such a process entailed leaving the Russians with the impression that they were free to invade countries in the Eastern *bloc* in circumstances when Russian security, even broadly defined, was not really in danger. The NATO declaration in the autumn of 1968 helped to make up for an earlier mistake—i.e. the mistake of believing that understandings about the political nature of the strategic *status quo* had been fully accepted by the Russians, and covered circumstances, such as those obtaining in Czechoslovakia, that the West Europeans deemed important if *détente* were to have much significance for them at all. By their declaration, the NATO Allies demonstrated a considerably more sophisticated attitude towards the relationship between a strategic *status quo* and political understanding than they had shown before. This was, potentially, a good sign of more effective progress in the future towards finding means of changing the pattern of confrontation in Europe and its essential political dimensions—although the pronouncement by Moscow in late 1968 of the so-called 'Brezhnev Doctrine', justifying Russian intervention in other socialist states, contrasted sharply with the conditions of behaviour demanded by the West European Allies as the price of pursuing *détente*.

The invasion of Czechoslovakia, and the events leading up to it, also exemplified a problem that had been the source of some anxiety in the West for several years. This was the whole question of how *détente* could progress, and include political changes in Eastern Europe, without these changes producing turmoil and a breakdown of all political and strategic understandings that had been reached during the two decades of confrontation. NATO and the Warsaw Pact would then form a context for change within a general sense of stability. There were essentially two schools of thought: first, that the continued existence of NATO would help to ensure that domestic disturbances in Eastern Europe did not bring about new East-West tensions and instability, and would reassure the Russians that change in Eastern Europe would not threaten stability across the East-West division; second, that the existence of

NATO—i.e. the continued existence of two armed camps dividing the Continent between them—would merely exacerbate the problem of change in Eastern Europe. This could happen if the Russians were led to hold down change because of fears that it would be exploited by the West. And this, in turn, would build up pressures for change that could lead to turmoil and internal conflict. On the other hand, the Russians might simply panic in the face of these internal changes and take foolish risks in the direction of the West.

The debate between these schools of thought was interrupted by the Soviet invasion of Czechoslovakia, which seemed to bear out the latter view: that the presence of NATO, rather than deterring the Russians from repression, actually heightened Russian concern lest the liberation movement in Czechoslovakia got out of hand. And the Russians seem to have defined their concept 'security' so broadly that it could preclude change of almost any sort, however unrelated to actual military security. By this standard, the situation in Czechoslovakia was indeed 'getting out of hand' from the Russian point of view. It may be argued that Russian behaviour was not really a realization of the fear that had sometimes been expressed in the West—namely, that a process of liberalization, once begun, would proceed too fast and inflame Soviet anxieties. It was rather that the continued presence of an armed context of confrontation had narrowed the scope of those changes that the Russians would be prepared to accept anywhere in the Eastern *bloc*. And, by this logic, the Soviet invasion of Czechoslovakia could not really have been prevented by threats from the West; only some reduction of the two armed camps in Europe would serve to broaden the scope of change in Eastern Europe acceptable to Moscow.

In so far as the armed context of confrontation actually influenced the Soviet decision to invade Czechoslovakia, this argument comes down to the proposition that the possibility of change in Eastern Europe—i.e. the emergence of the conditions under which *détente* will have some meaning for Western

Europeans—can only occur after real efforts have been made to reduce the dependence of the present confrontation on armaments and troops. In other words, it is possible that change in Eastern Europe would be more acceptable to the Russians were it not for the mass of NATO and Warsaw Pact forces facing one another. This view may be over-optimistic, though it is not implausible or inconsistent. However, one can only really say that the Soviet invasion seems to indicate that the Russians will go to some lengths to preserve political influence and the communist system in Eastern Europe. Unfortunately, there has been no way of testing this proposition about the two *blocs*, and the considered reaction by the NATO Powers to the invasion—not the initial acceptance of it—seems to make it even less likely that a process of reducing the role of armaments in confrontation will be begun soon. It may be that the warning issued by the NATO Powers to the Russians about similar behaviour in Eastern Europe was the right approach to take— a deterrent approach—in an effort to get the Russians to accept the conditions necessary for *détente*. But in a longer view, it might prove to have been the wrong approach if the question is really one of reducing the element of force remaining in East-West relations as fast as possible in order to bring about the conditions for Eastern European liberalization. This proposition, too, cannot be demonstrated without being tested.

This discussion illustrates a further point about *détente*— namely, the difficulty of determining what steps will lead from the present arrangements for security in Europe to some new political position, in which there will be less dependence upon forces and a greater degree of political and economic contact throughout the whole of Europe. How will it be possible to reduce forces on both sides in Europe, given the political climate prevailing in Western Europe after the invasion of Czechoslovakia? Here, again, the response of NATO is significant. The use of a military instrument—including appeals for limited increases in force levels—in order to give diplomatic signals, shows how difficult it would be to change a military-political context back into a strictly political context. In this sense, the use of a military means of signalling may have been unfortunate: it may only have helped to delay any serious consideration of the problems entailed in ending the formalism of that military context, or of reducing the forces that are physically in position and making the change even more difficult.

Beginning in the mid-1960s, the NATO powers gave some consideration to a process of 'mutual and balanced force reductions' *vis-à-vis* the Warsaw Pact powers. This consideration has never got very far, although it is still perhaps too early to tell whether the force 'redeployments' by NATO will eventually find a 'mutual and balanced' response by the Russians, despite the political uses to which Russian forces were being put in Czechoslovakia even in 1969. The question of force reductions in Europe has also always begged certain central questions, such as the role of Soviet forces in East Germany in supporting a régime that has needed support at least in part because of the failure of the West to recognize its legitimacy. In other words, 'mutual and balanced force reductions' have failed in part because the West wanted to accomplish two contradictory purposes at the same time: to take steps that would advance a concept of *détente* and reduce the military residue of the Cold War, yet at the same time to deny the demands of *détente* to a country that definitely exists as an economic and political unit and, indeed, has exerted considerable influence in the East to stifle change—as it did by promoting the invasion of Czechoslovakia—in part because it is denied the legitimacy that is granted the Government in Bonn even by the Soviet Union.

It is a matter of choice: yet if there were a possibility of real force reductions on both sides—thereby creating one of the major conditions for a real reconstitution of European politics —then the burden of argument would seem to lie with the recognition of East Germany by the West. Indeed, the debate on this problem has always been somewhat artificial—i.e., East Germany is a 'fact', and failure in the West to affirm it is one of the strongest forces acting against change in the East and for continuation of anxieties, real or manufactured, in Eastern Europe and the Soviet Union about West Germany and Western intentions in general. Therefore, recognition of the Pankow regime by the West may even be the best way for the West Germans to gain, step by step, the 'reunification' that is impossible so long as an East German Government has to search so desperately for legitimacy.

This problem of East Germany is but one example of the tremendous complications involved in the search for *détente*—and, indeed, in every consideration of European security and change—which have been posed by the anomalous status of Germany. These complications increased in 1955 when both Germanies were formally included in the context of military confrontation in Europe. And ever since then, even leaving aside the diplomatic problems in both East and West and the difficulties, mostly in the West, of arriving at common Alliance positions on anything, the question of Germany has remained central to any concept of a reconstituted pattern of security on the Continent. Indeed, American involvement on the Continent remains as important as ever, if only to reassure everyone—including the West Germans—about the West Germans' good behaviour. The United States remains the primary West European power charged with providing security against Germany as well as against the Soviet Union, and has had its role emphasized by the departure of de Gaulle.

The basic question is simple: where would a reunited Germany stand—in the West or in the East? Certainly, if a reunited Germany were to gravitate to one direction, there would be no strategic value in *détente* for the other side. Indeed, there would most likely be a crisis of extreme proportions in reaction to such a radical disturbance of the strategic balance.

On the other hand, could not Germany simply be reunified and left as a neutral country in the centre of a Europe still divided between NATO and the Warsaw Pact? Since the context of conflict has included the idea of two Germanies for so long, and since weapons' policies, troops' deployments, strategies, and diplomatic relations both within NATO and the Warsaw Pact have for so long been based on the existence of two Germanies and on the integration of the Federal Republic and Democratic Republic in their respective Alliances, this solution also seems unthinkable. It might have been possible if both Germanies had been kept out of the two alliance systems —or if the process of tidying up the loose ends in Germany in 1947–48 had not led to a formalization of Germany's division. But that time is long since past.

A third alternative is perhaps the most promising: namely to find a means for a reunified Germany to take its place within a Europe that is itself no longer divided. This seems to be the goal: to unify the Continent without that process benefiting either the Russians or the Americans strategically, and without its meaning the extension of the political influence of either super-power into today's strategic sphere of the other at the other's expense.

Within such a context, the role of one Germany, two Germanies, or even of twelve would no longer be paramount. Indeed, for safety's sake, there could conceivably be two semi-sovereign Germanies, reunified in everything but name as a result of a prolonged process of functional co-operation. There would still remain the problems posed by attempts of a Western social-democratic country more or less to amalgamate with a communist one, but—when Ulbricht departs—that should not necessarily prove an insuperable obstacle, provided some means could be found to ensure that the new arrangements would not upset the strategic *status quo* or the balance of political influence in Europe.

The search for such a means to preserve the strategic *status quo* in Europe and the balance of political influence will, of course, involve an active role to be played by the nations of the Warsaw Pact, regardless of the direction taken by *détente*. But what will this role be? At the moment, the answer to this question must remain somewhat obscure, if only because of the extremely broad terms in which the Soviet Union has chosen to define its own 'security'. This Soviet attitude has given a false air of cohesion to the Eastern *bloc* Alliance that would hardly be evident if there were a general erosion of both NATO and the Warsaw Pact, without the retention of some equivalent means, such as the network of Soviet bilateral treaties, to enable Moscow to retain close control over the foreign and domestic political development of its Allies.

But despite the limited political influence of the East European Allies within the context of the Warsaw Pact—especially since the Brezhnev Doctrine has introduced new uncertainties concerning the possible Russian response to change in these states—there remain some major identities of interest among most of the Warsaw Pact powers concerning the terms of any possible restructuring of European security. It is not just the greater geographical cohesion of the Pact as compared to NATO; nor is it just the fears of West Germany, real or artificial, that are evident within the Northern Tier nations in the Pact. It is also a recognition that the Soviet Union is in no position to choose a policy of isolating itself from the European continent: it is rooted there by geography and by the memory that policy during the inter-war years—from Rapallo and the *cordon sanitaire* imposed by the West to the Nazi-Soviet Pact—failed to provide the Soviet Union with any lasting security.

Partly because of this understanding about the necessary involvement of the Soviet Union in problems of European security, there has never been a real crisis of confidence in Eastern Europe about the willingness of the Soviet Union to use nuclear weapons on its Allies' behalf. And there is also no practical way for the Eastern *bloc* states to contemplate new patterns of European security that do not take a greater notice of Russian attitudes than would be necessary for West European states in relation to American attitudes. Even Roumania has been somewhat more circumspect in its challenges to the Russian Alliance —in its security aspects—than the French under President de Gaulle have been with regard to the American Alliance.

At the same time, however, there is a greater sense within Eastern Europe that forms of independence, sought in order to pursue national policies of internal development, are more likely to be realized within the context of a Europe that is not so closely dependent upon the military trappings of two military *blocs*. Even if these developments continued to be closely monitored by the Soviet Union, most East European states would prefer to have this arranged on a bilateral basis rather than as a by-product of a military confrontation with the West which itself could increase Soviet anxieties about internal change.

For some time, therefore, there has been considerable support in the Eastern *bloc* for the diplomatic initiatives taken by the Warsaw Pact—initiatives directed towards dissolving both NATO and the Pact, itself. In the past perhaps, this concern has also reflected the strategic advantages the Soviet Union would enjoy over the United States in an undivided Europe, because of the former's closer geographical proximity to Central Europe. But now that some basic understandings seem to have been achieved concerning at least the strategic division of the Continent, there is concern in the East as well as in the West to see European security restructured on a basis that does not require such a high level of costly forces. And such changes would also fit within the general Russian attitude that the settling of political differences can be a means to achieve stability—in contrast to the greater emphasis placed by the Americans on stability that derives from 'strategic' balances—although Moscow might still attempt to use such a process to gain a more important political position in Europe, both East and West.

It is within this context that specific proposals advanced by the Warsaw Pact powers should be seen. Perhaps the most important of these proposals—for a European Security Conference—was contained in the communiqué of the Pact's Political Consultative Committee, issued following its meeting in Bucharest in the summer of 1966 (see Appendix V). This proposal was repeated in roughly similar terms after the Warsaw Pact summit in Budapest in March 1969. But even in 1966 the idea was not new: as early as 1954, the Soviet Union had tried to forestall both West Germany's entry into a Western Alliance and the final act of formally dividing Europe that this step represented. At that time, the proposal was firmly rejected by the West.

The Warsaw Pact proposal in 1966, that a general European Security Conference should be held, was not simply a gesture which recognized that there was a condition of strategic *status quo* prevailing across the Continent. Indeed, it was obviously conceived very much with the problem of West Germany in mind, at a time when the 'nuclear sharing' issue in NATO had hardly begun to disappear. And the Warsaw Pact initiative also seemed to represent attempts to exploit divisions in NATO following the withdrawal of France from Allied Command Europe. But despite these ambiguous motives, there was a strong sense in the 1966 communiqué of a hard-headed view of security problems—namely, that the continuation of East and West German armies and of two armed camps, in general, could actually increase political uncertainties and perhaps even pose threats to the continuation of European security, itself.

On the face of it, this concept is not very far from that later advanced by the NATO nations when they called for 'mutual and balanced force reductions'. The difference lies both in the scope of the two approaches—on the one hand a formal conference to discuss political problems, and on the other a series of careful steps limited at first to the military realm—and in Western suspicion of the intentions of the Eastern *bloc* states. Again, the essential barrier to a common approach has been the 'German problem': that is, the Warsaw Pact proposal entails formal acceptance of the German Democratic Republic by the West, a condition that is still unacceptable to NATO.

Yet there still remains something of value in the proposal for a European Security Conference, especially in the recognition that this would only be part of a long process. In particular, in the words of the 1966 communiqué, there could be progress even if the NATO nations were not yet ready for a 'complete dissolution of both alignments', and the process could begin with an 'understanding on the abolition' of both military organizations; bilateral or multilateral efforts to advance the 'cause of European security'; and the taking of 'partial measures towards military relaxation on the European continent'.

NATO has found it difficult to come to terms with these proposals partly because of the lack of symmetry in the strategic positions of the two alliances. The 'partial measures' referred to, for example, included a nuclear-free zone, reduction of German forces on both sides, an end to foreign war bases, and withdrawal of foreign forces to 'within their national frontiers'. And despite the appeal these proposals would have even for a nation like Roumania—which has sought withdrawal of Russian forces stationed in Eastern Europe—the strategic advantage in all of them still lies with the Soviet Union.

This, of course, has been a weakness central to almost every proposal for changing patterns of confrontation in Europe— i.e. how does one get from A to B without there being an advantage conferred to one side or the other because of the basic assymetry of their strategic positions and, more particularly, of the political roles played by military forces in the internal politics of the two alliances.

But at least the 1966 communiqué of the Warsaw Pact powers implicitly conceded one essential point: namely that the Americans could participate in the process of restructuring security in Europe. This was a major step—which seems to have been included in the 1969 Budapest declaration as well. It creates a framework in which both the Soviet Union and the United States can be seen as joint guarantors of whatever new system of security is evolved for Europe. Yet despite this hopeful sign that the Warsaw Pact states are concerned to take steps that recognize basic strategic and political requirements, there is still no clear method, even within the context of a European

Security Conference, of resolving the many dilemmas posed by any effort to change today's patterns of confrontation.

In addition, there is a sense in which the Warsaw Pact declarations of Bucharest in 1966 and Budapest in 1969 can be seen as serving internal needs of the Pact—as instruments of anti-Western propaganda—in conjunction with the Soviet view of the limits to be placed on liberalization in Eastern Europe. Both documents, for example, contain references to East-West contacts, and appear to sanction them: namely, 'the strengthening of economic and trade relations, the multiplication of contacts and forms of co-operation' (1966); and to 'strengthen political, economic, and cultural contacts' (1969). On the face of it, these statements fit neatly within the concept of *détente* as it has become important for the West European states. But are these really efforts to legitimize East-West contacts, or are they merely a formal expression of the limits placed by the Soviet Union on the range of activities permitted to the Eastern *bloc* states? The very facts of the Soviet invasion of Czechoslovakia and the enunciation of the Brezhnev Doctrine —both coming between the Bucharest and Budapest declarations—seem to support the latter view.

Despite this pessimistic view of Soviet intentions, however, there is considerable merit in the view that the NATO powers should accept the Warsaw Pact invitation to hold a European Security Conference—as, indeed, several of the smaller NATO countries have urged their larger Allies to do. Most important, such a conference would open direct contacts between individual states in Eastern Europe and NATO countries. And having supported the idea of a European Security Conference in the first place, the Soviet Union would find it difficult to deny the legitimacy of these contacts—contacts that have been limited by Soviet policy since the invasion of Czechoslovakia. For the same reason, there is much to be said for the creation of a permanent European Security Commission, to be composed of all states concerned with the future of Europe. Such a commission could also legitimize an increase in East-West contacts even if it did little to sort out problems specifically concerned with European security.

These would be only tentative steps, however. It is still hard to see how it would be possible in the near future for a process of *détente* to lead to basic changes in the nature of confrontation in Europe. This is so partly because of the internal problems faced by the Warsaw Pact and, in particular, because of the broad Soviet definition of its own security requirements. Yet even assuming that these problems could be sorted out to the satisfaction of all Europeans, both East and West—and in this context the Americans must qualify as Europeans—it is hard to see a context emerging in the near future in which the role of the military *blocs* could be reduced, and then eliminated, without there arising significant difficulties concerning the means of sharing political influence in Europe between the two super-powers.

At present, there is no clear picture of an undivided Europe in which the influence of the United States and that of the Soviet Union could be carefully controlled, unless, perhaps, this undivided Europe itself gained a high degree of unity and became a significant power in its own right. But this is not a very likely possibility politically, or in view of the strategic implications it could have: neither the Americans nor the Russians would be particularly comfortable with a strong and united Europe spanning the Continent that would inevitably favour one of today's super-powers at the expense of the other.

But if the problem of controlling an encroachment of either Russian or American influence across the agreed line of division would create difficulties in a unified Europe, at least concepts exist of Europe's strategic unity. Europe could, quite simply, become a continent in which there was sufficient American and Soviet agreement about the ground-rules of the strategic *status quo* for them to act as mutual guarantors of a disarmed Europe; one no longer divided, one protected against internecine strife and the possibility of a threat to 'security' from one or more Germanies.

This idea may sound too utopian. And experience with schemes like the League of Nations and the United Nations lead to caution. But it must be remembered that the United States and the Soviet Union have managed to sort out a wide range of their differences in Europe, at least those expressed in strategic terms, and they will in the foreseeable future undoubtedly continue to retain important interests in the Continent. These interests will almost surely lead them to define their common interests in a far better way than was the case among the League powers, or between America and Russia at the UN in 1945. In these earlier cases, there was almost no commonly accepted understanding about the strategic or political guidelines shaping great power relations on the Continent. And, finally, the nature of warfare and of super-power relations in the nuclear age will almost certainly ensure that America and Russia are powers to be reckoned with in European affairs into the indefinite future. No new isolationism is now really possible for either country.

The concept of a disarmed, mutually guaranteed Europe is not at all implausible—and within it, the dominant problem of Germany could cease to have the importance it has today. But, again the problem with this and other models of a Europe of the future lies in getting from A to B—from here to there. Some of the problems of mutual force reductions have already been pointed out. And the experience of Czechoslovakia in 1968 certainly indicates that, in matters concerning the relative influence of the super-powers in the two halves of Europe after a dissolution of formal military confrontation, the Russians have up till now not been very encouraging. This is true whatever their motives for the invasion of Czechoslovakia. In short, the means if not the ends of changing the pattern of confrontation in Europe now seem to be less attainable. And in the wake of this invasion, one can discern a greater uneasiness in Western Europe about the possibility that the Russians and Americans will conduct a dialogue on the future of the whole Continent over the heads of their Allies. One can also sense increased concern about the importance of national nuclear weapons systems in Europe, which could preserve some options for these nations, whatever the Americans and Russians attempt to construct on the Continent. It is arguable that the security of all parties interested in the future of Europe might be greatly increased if some ideal model such as the one outlined above were to be brought into being. But the uncertainties of the process of making that model real—a process that was made even more uncertain by the invasion of Czechoslovakia—are likely to bring responses from European nations which, at every step of the way, would, in terms of security, vastly complicate any progress to a Europe that is substantially different from the one we see today.

For the indefinite future, therefore, it seems that NATO and the Warsaw Pact will remain largely as they are now, enshrining an obsolete pattern of confrontation in Europe; and continuing a context of military confrontation that has no real meaning any longer. Even the aftermath of the Czech invasion has shown this: there was no increase in the perception of a Soviet 'threat' to Western Europe, and no Western reaction to any such perception. But, in lacking the means to get from one situation of strategic stability to another that would be vastly preferable by practically any criterion, both the NATO and the Warsaw Pact states have chosen to see the military organs remain, largely unimpaired and unready to consider real alternatives. As in the early days of this military confrontation, the formal institutions continue to dominate political patterns of behaviour, and they will probably continue to do so; and— as the invasion of Czechoslovakia seems to indicate—there will most likely be gradual approaches to change, interspersed with setbacks, hopefully getting ever closer to some concept of a different means of organizing security and political relations on the Continent. Perhaps, suddenly one day, everyone will realize that the patterns of confrontation have changed in the course of this process, and NATO and the Warsaw Pact will just wither away.

Alternatively, there will be a succession of false starts that founder on the complications of trying to cause change while at the same time accepting the existence of the two alliances. Eventually, political relations across the present division may develop to a point where the two fully-armed military camps come to be seen as complete anachronisms, irrelevant to the political and strategic problems of the Continent. At that point, all the nations concerned with the future of Europe may construct an entirely new system of security in one grand effort.

Whichever of these alternatives comes to pass—or other possibilities not yet seen—NATO and the Warsaw Pact are likely to be with us for some time, with their internal needs and parochial concerns, and with the continuing patterns of Alliance politics that they create. This may not be a very optimistic forecast, but then this system of security has provided an era significant in modern European history without a major war. To abandon such a system—whatever its tensions and problems—without first finding something substantially better to put in its place, might itself be the surest means of denying Europe its present hopes for a future of real and lasting security.

The Brussels Treaty

17 March 1948

The titular heads of the participating States:
Resolved to reaffirm their faith in fundamental human rights, in the dignity and worth of the human person and in the other ideals proclaimed in the Charter of the United Nations; To fortify and preserve the principles of democracy, personal freedom and political liberty, the constitutional traditions and the rule of law, which are their common heritage; To strengthen, with these aims in view, the economic, social and cultural ties by which they are already united; To co-operate loyally and to co-ordinate their efforts to create in Western Europe a firm basis for European economic recovery;

To afford assistance to each other, in accordance with the Charter of the United Nations, in maintaining international peace and security and in resisting any policy of aggression; To take such steps as may be held to be necessary in the event of a renewal by Germany of a policy of aggression; To associate progressively in the pursuance of these aims other States inspired by the same ideals and animated by the like determination;

Desiring for these purposes to conclude a treaty for collaboration in economic, social and cultural matters and for collective self-defence;

Have appointed ... their plenipotentiaries ... who ... have agreed as follows:

ARTICLE I

Convinced of the close community of their interests and of the necessity of uniting in order to promote the economic recovery of Europe, the High Contracting Parties will so organize and co-ordinate their economic activities as to produce the best possible results, by the elimination of conflict in their economic policies, the co-ordination of production and the development of commercial exchanges.

The co-operation provided for in the preceding paragraph, which will be effected through the Consultative Council referred to in Article VII as well as through other bodies, shall not involve any duplication of, or prejudice to, the work of other economic organizations in which the High Contracting Parties are or may be represented but shall on the contrary assist the work of those organizations.

ARTICLE II

The High Contracting Parties will make every effort in common, both by direct consultation and in specialized agencies, to promote the attainment of a higher standard of living by their peoples and to develop on corresponding lines the social and other related services of their countries.

The High Contracting Parties will consult with the object of achieving the earliest possible application of recommendations of immediate practical interest, relating to social matters, adopted with their approval in the specialized agencies.

They will endeavour to conclude as soon as possible conventions with each other in the sphere of social security.

ARTICLE III

The High Contracting Parties will make every effort in common to lead their peoples towards a better understanding of the principles which form the basis of their common civilization and to promote cultural exchanges by conventions between themselves or by other means.

ARTICLE IV

If any of the High Contracting Parties should be the object of an armed attack in Europe, the other High Contracting Parties will, in accordance with the provisions of Article 51 of the Charter of the United Nations, afford the Party so attacked all the military and other aid and assistance in their power.

ARTICLE V

All measures taken as a result of the preceding Article shall be immediately reported to the Security Council. They shall be terminated as soon as the Security Council has taken the measures necessary to maintain or restore international peace and security.

The present Treaty does not prejudice in any way the obligations of the High Contracting Parties under the provisions of the Charter of the United Nations. It shall not be interpreted as affecting in any way the authority and responsibility of the Security Council under the Charter to take at any time such action as it deems necessary in order to maintain or restore international peace and security.

ARTICLE VI

The High Contracting Parties declare, each so far as he is concerned, that none of the international engagements now in force between him and any of the other High Contracting Parties or any third State is in conflict with the provisions of the present Treaty.

None of the High Contracting Parties will conclude any alliance or participate in any coalition directed against any other of the High Contracting Parties.

ARTICLE VII

For the purpose of consulting together on all the questions dealt with in the present Treaty, the High Contracting Parties will create a Consultative Council, which shall be so organized as to be able to exercise its functions continuously. The Council shall meet at such times as it shall deem fit.

At the request of any of the High Contracting Parties, the Council shall be immediately convened in order to permit the High Contracting Parties to consult with regard to any situation which may constitute a threat to peace, in whatever area this threat should arise; with regard to the attitude to be adopted and the steps to be taken in case of a renewal by Germany of an aggressive policy; or with regard to any situation constituting a danger to economic stability.

ARTICLE VIII

In pursuance of their determination to settle disputes only by peaceful means, the High Contracting Parties will apply to disputes between themselves the following provision:

The High Contracting Parties will, while the present Treaty remains in force, settle all disputes falling within the scope of Article 36, paragraph 2, of the Statute of the International Court of Justice by referring them to the Court ...

ARTICLE IX

The High Contracting Parties may, by agreement, invite any other State to accede to the present Treaty on conditions to be agreed between them and the State so invited . . .

ARTICLE X

The present Treaty . . . shall enter into force on the date of the deposit of the last instrument of ratification and shall thereafter remain in force for fifty years . . .

Done at Brussels, this seventeenth day of March, 1948 . . .

Appendix II

The North Atlantic Treaty

Washington D.C., 4 April 1949[1]

The Parties to this Treaty reaffirm their faith in the purposes and principles of the Charter of the United Nations and their desire to live in peace with all peoples and all Governments.

They are determined to safeguard the freedom, common heritage and civilization of their peoples, founded on the principles of democracy, individual liberty and the rule of law.

They seek to promote stability and well-being in the North Atlantic area.

They are resolved to unite their efforts for collective defence and for the preservation of peace and security.

They therefore agree to this North Atlantic Treaty:

ARTICLE I

The Parties undertake, as set forth in the Charter of the United Nations, to settle any international dispute in which they may be involved by peaceful means in such a manner that international peace and security and justice are not endangered, and to refrain in their international relations from the threat or use of force in any manner inconsistent with the purposes of the United Nations.

ARTICLE II

The Parties will contribute toward the further development of peaceful and friendly international relations by strengthening their free institutions, by bringing about a better understanding of the principles upon which these institutions are founded, and by promoting conditions of stability and wellbeing. They will seek to eliminate conflict in their international economic policies and will encourage economic collaboration between any or all of them.

---

[1] The Treaty came into force on 24 August, 1949, after the deposition of the ratifications of all signatory states.

ARTICLE III

In order more effectively to achieve the objectives of this Treaty, the Parties, separately and jointly, by means of continuous and effective self-help and mutual aid, will maintain and develop their individual and collective capacity to resist armed attack.

ARTICLE IV

The Parties will consult together whenever, in the opinion of any of them, the territorial integrity, political independence or security of any of the Parties is threatened.

ARTICLE V

The Parties agree that an armed attack against one or more of them in Europe or North America shall be considered an attack against them all and consequently they agree that, if such an armed attack occurs, each of them, in exercise of the right of individual or collective self-defence recognized by Article 51 of the Charter of the United Nations, will assist the Party or Parties so attacked by taking forthwith, individually and in concert with the other Parties, such action as it deems necessary, including the use of armed force, to restore and maintain the security of the North Atlantic area.

Any such armed attack and all measures taken as a result thereof shall immediately be reported to the Security Council. Such measures shall be terminated when the Security Council has taken the measures necessary to restore and maintain international peace and security.

ARTICLE VI[1]

For the purpose of Article V, an armed attack on one or more of the Parties is deemed to include an armed attack
   —on the territory of any of the Parties in Europe or North America, on the Algerian Departments of France,[2] on the territory of Turkey or on the islands under the jurisdiction of

[1] As amended by Article 2 of the Protocol to the North Atlantic Treaty on the accession of Greece and Turkey.

[2] On 16 January, 1963, the French Representative made a statement to the North Atlantic Council on the effects of the independence of Algeria on certain aspects of the North Atlantic Treaty. The Council noted that in so far as the former Algerian Departments of France were concerned the relevant clauses of this Treaty had become inapplicable as from 3 July, 1962.

any of the Parties in the North Atlantic area north of the Tropic
of Cancer;

—on the forces, vessels, or aircraft of any of the Parties, when in
or over these territories or any other area in Europe in which
occupation forces of any of the Parties were stationed on the
date when the Treaty entered into force or the Mediterranean
Sea or in the North Atlantic area north of the Tropic of Cancer.

ARTICLE VII

This Treaty does not affect, and shall not be interpreted as affecting,
in any way the rights and obligations under the Charter of the
Parties which are members of the United Nations, or the primary
responsibility of the Security Council for the maintenance of international peace and security.

ARTICLE VIII

Each Party declares that none of the international engagements now
in force between it and any other of the Parties or any third State is
in conflict with the provisions of this Treaty, and undertakes not to
enter into any international engagement in conflict with this Treaty.

ARTICLE IX

The Parties hereby establish a Council, on which each of them shall
be represented to consider matters concerning the implementation
of this Treaty. The Council shall be so organized as to be able to
meet promptly at any time. The Council shall set up such subsidiary
bodies as may be necessary; in particular it shall establish immediately a defence committee which shall recommend measures for
the implementation of Articles 3 and 5.

ARTICLE X

The Parties may, by unanimous agreement, invite any other
European State in a position to further the principles of this Treaty
and to contribute to the security of the North Atlantic area to
accede to this Treaty. Any State so invited may become a party to
the Treaty by depositing its instrument of accession with the Government of the United States of America. The Government of the
United States of America will inform each of the Parties of the
deposit of each such instrument of accession.

ARTICLE XI

This Treaty shall be ratified and its provisions carried out by the Parties in accordance with their respective constitutional processes. The instruments of ratification shall be deposited as soon as possible with the Government of the United States of America, which will notify all the other signatories of each deposit. The Treaty shall enter into force between the States which have ratified it as soon as the ratifications of the majority of the signatories, including the ratifications of Belgium, Canada, France, Luxembourg, the Netherlands, the United Kingdom and the United States, have been deposited and shall come into effect with respect to other States on the date of the deposit of their ratifications.

ARTICLE XII

After the Treaty has been in force for ten years, or at any time thereafter, the Parties shall, if any of them so requests, consult together for the purpose of reviewing the Treaty, having regard for the factors then affecting peace and security in the North Atlantic area, including the development of universal as well as regional arrangements under the Charter of the United Nations for the maintenance of international peace and security.

ARTICLE XIII

After the Treaty has been in force for twenty years, any Party may cease to be a Party one year after its notice of denunciation has been given to the Government of the United States of America, which will inform the Governments of the other Parties of the deposit of each notice of denunciation.

ARTICLE XIV

This Treaty, of which the English and French texts are equally authentic, shall be deposited in the archives of the Government of the United States of America. Duly certified copies will be transmitted by that Government to the Governments of the other signatories.

Appendix III

Treaty of Friendship, Co-operation and Mutual Assistance[1]

Warsaw, 14 May 1955

PREAMBLE

The Contracting Parties, reaffirming their desire for the establish-ment of a system of European collective security based on the participation of all European states irrespective of their social and political systems, which would make it possible to unite their efforts in safeguarding the peace of Europe:

mindful, at the same time, of the situation created in Europe by the ratification of the Paris agreements, which envisage the forma-tion of a new military alignment in the shape of 'Western European Union', with the participation of a remilitarized Western Germany and the integration of the latter in the North Atlantic *bloc*, which increases the danger of another war and constitutes a threat to the national security of peaceable states;

being persuaded that in these circumstances the peaceable European states must take the necessary measures to safeguard their security and in the interests of preserving peace in Europe;

guided by the objects and principles of the Charter of the United Nations Organization;

being desirous of further promoting and developing friendship, co-operation and mutual assistance in accordance with the principles of respect for the independence and sovereignty of states and of non-interference in their internal affairs;

have decided to conclude the present Treaty of Friendship, Co-operation and Mutual Assistance and have for that purpose ap-pointed as their plenipotentiaries; (follow the names of the pleni-potentiaries of Albania, Bulgaria, Hungary, East Germany, Poland, Roumania, the Soviet Union and Czechoslovakia), who, having presented their full powers, found in good and due form, have agreed as follows:

[1] Translation published in *New Times*, No. 21, 21 May, 1955 (Moscow).

ARTICLE I

The Contracting Parties undertake, in accordance with the Charter of the United Nations Organization, to refrain in their international relations from the threat or use of force, and to settle their international disputes peacefully and in such manner as will not jeopardize international peace and security.

ARTICLE II

The Contracting Parties declare their readiness to participate in a spirit of sincere co-operation in all international actions designed to safeguard international peace and security, and will fully devote their energies to the attainment of this end.

The Contracting Parties will furthermore strive for the adoption, in agreement with other states which may desire to co-operate in this, of effective measures for universal reduction of armaments and prohibition of atomic, hydrogen and other weapons of mass destruction.

ARTICLE III

The Contracting Parties shall consult with one another on all important international issues affecting their common interests, guided by the desire to strengthen international peace and security.

They shall immediately consult with one another whenever, in the opinion of any one of them, a threat of armed attack on one or more of the Parties to the Treaty has arisen, in order to ensure joint defence and the maintenance of peace and security.

ARTICLE IV

In the event of armed attack in Europe on one or more of the Parties to the Treaty by any state or group of states, each of the Parties to the Treaty, in the exercise of its right to individual or collective self-defence, in accordance with Article 51 of the Charter of the United Nations Organization, shall immediately, either individually or in agreement with other Parties to the Treaty, come to the assistance of the state or states attacked with all such means as it deems necessary, including armed force. The Parties to the Treaty shall immediately consult concerning the necessary measures to be taken by them jointly in order to restore and maintain international peace and security.

Measures taken on the basis of this Article shall be reported to the Security Council in conformity with the provisions of the Charter of the United Nations Organization. These measures shall be discontinued immediately the Security Council adopts the necessary measures to restore and maintain international peace and security.

ARTICLE V

The Contracting Parties have agreed to establish a Joint Command of the armed forces that by agreement among the Parties shall be assigned to the Command, which shall function on the basis of jointly established principles. They shall likewise adopt other agreed measures necessary to strengthen their defensive power, in order to protect the peaceful labours of their peoples, guarantee the inviolability of their frontiers and territories, and provide defence against possible aggression.

ARTICLE VI

For the purpose of the consultations among the Parties envisaged in the present Treaty, and also for the purpose of examining questions which may arise in the operation of the Treaty, a Political Consultatives' Committee shall be set up, in which each of the Parties to the Treaty shall be represented by a member of its Government or by another specifically appointed representative.

The Committee may set up such auxiliary bodies as may prove necessary.

ARTICLE VII

The Contracting Parties undertake not to participate in any coalitions or alliances and not to conclude any agreements whose objects conflict with the objects of the present Treaty.

The Contracting Parties declare that their commitments under existing international treaties do not conflict with the provisions of the present Treaty.

ARTICLE VIII

The Contracting Parties declare that they will act in a spirit of friendship and co-operation with a view to further developing and fostering economic and cultural relations with one another, each adhering to the principle of respect for the independence and sovereignty of the others and non-interference in their internal affairs.

ARTICLE IX

The present Treaty is open to the accession of other states irrespective of their social and political systems, which express their readiness by participation in the present Treaty to assist in uniting the efforts of the peaceable states in safeguarding the peace and security of the peoples. Such accession shall enter into force with the agreement of the Parties to the Treaty after the declaration of accession has been deposited with the Government of the Polish People's Republic.

ARTICLE X

The present Treaty is subject to ratification, and the instruments of ratification shall be deposited with the Government of the Polish People's Republic.

The Treaty shall enter into force on the day the last instrument of ratification has been deposited. The Government of the Polish People's Republic shall notify the other Parties to the Treaty as each instrument of ratification is deposited.

ARTICLE XI

The present Treaty shall remain in force for twenty years. For such Contracting Parties as do not one year before the expiration of this period present to the Government of the Polish People's Republic a statement of denunciation of the Treaty, it shall remain in force for the next ten years.

Should a system of collective security be established in Europe, and a General European Treaty of Collective Security concluded for this purpose, for which the Contracting Parties will unswervingly strive, the present Treaty shall cease to be operative from the day the General European Treaty enters into force.

Done in Warsaw on 14 May, 1955, in one copy each in the Russian, Polish, Czech and German languages, all texts being equally authentic. Certified copies of the present Treaty shall be sent by the Government of the Polish People's Republic to all the Parties to the Treaty.

In witness thereof the plenipotentiaries have signed the present Treaty and affixed their seals.

Security in Europe

Communiqué on the

ESTABLISHMENT OF A JOINT COMMAND

of the Armed Forces of the Signatories to the Treaty of Friendship, Co-operation and Mutual Assistance

Warsaw, 14 May, 1955

In pursuance of the Treaty of Friendship, Co-operation and Mutual Assistance between the People's Republic of Albania, the People's Republic of Bulgaria, the Hungarian People's Republic, the German Democratic Republic, the Polish People's Republic, the Roumanian People's Republic, the Union of Soviet Socialist Republics and the Czechoslovak Republic, the signatory states have decided to establish a Joint Command of their armed forces.

The decision provides that general questions relating to the strengthening of the defensive power and the organization of the Joint Armed Forces of the signatory states shall be subject to examination by the Political Consultative Committee, which shall adopt the necessary decisions.

Marshal of the Soviet Union I. S. Konev has been appointed Commander-in-Chief of the Joint Armed Forces to be assigned by the signatory states.

The Ministers of Defence or other military leaders of the signatory states are to serve as Deputy Commanders-in-Chief of the Joint Armed Forces, and shall command the armed forces assigned by their respective states to the Joint Armed Forces.

The question of the participation of the German Democratic Republic in measures concerning the armed forces of the Joint Command will be examined at a later date.

A Staff of the Joint Armed Forces of the signatory states will be set up under the Commander-in-Chief of the Joint Armed Forces, and will include permanent representatives of the General Staffs of the signatory states.

The Staff will have its headquarters in Moscow.

The disposition of the Joint Armed Forces in the territories of the signatory states will be effected, by agreement among the states, in accordance with the requirements of their mutual defence.

Appendix IV

General de Gaulle's Press Conference (extracts)

21 February 1966

Nothing can cause a law that is no longer in accord with custom to remain in force unamended. Nothing can cause a treaty to remain wholly valid once its purpose has altered. Nothing can cause an alliance to continue as it stands when the conditions in which it was created have changed: The law, the treaty, the alliance must be adapted to the new situation; otherwise such texts, denuded of substance, will, when need arises, be no more than empty words on paper—unless there occurs some brutal rupture between these outdated forms and the living reality.

While France believes that it is today still useful for her security and for that of the West that she should be allied to a certain number of States, and to America in particular, for their defence and for her own in case of aggression against one of them; while the joint declaration in this respect, which took the form of the Atlantic Alliance Treaty signed in Washington on 4 April 1949, remains valid in her eyes she also recognizes that the measures which were subsequently taken to apply it no longer meet the new situation in what, so far as she is concerned, is a satisfactory manner.

I said, 'the new situation'. It is, indeed, clear that as a result of the interior and exterior evolution of the countries of the East, the Western world is today no longer threatened as it was at the time when the American protectorate was organized in Europe under the cover of NATO. But as our fears became less sharp, there was at the same time occurring a reduction in what had been an as good as absolute guarantee of security, bestowed upon the Old Continent by America's exclusive possession of atomic weapons and by the certitude that she would use them without restriction in case of aggression. For, since that time, Soviet Russia has equipped herself with nuclear weapons capable of striking directly at the United States, and this has, at the very least, made the American decision regarding the use of their bombs uncertain, and has, at the same time—I am speaking for France—taken away the justification, not indeed for the Alliance, but for integration.

On the other hand, while the likelihood of a world war breaking out on Europe's account is decreasing, conflicts in which America is engaged in other parts of the world—the day before yesterday in Korea, yesterday in Cuba, today in Vietnam—by virtue of the famous escalation principle, risk assuming dimensions which could lead to a general conflagration. In that event, Europe, whose strategy within NATO is that of America, would be automatically drawn into the struggle she had not sought. And this would be true for France, if the inclusion in the military system under American command of her territory, her communications, certain of her forces, many of her air bases, and some of her ports, were to be further prolonged. Into the bargain, our country is becoming on its own account and by its own means an atomic power, and is thus led to take upon itself the very wide political and strategic responsibilities implied by this capability, the nature and scope of which render them obviously inalienable. Finally, France's will to be responsible for her own destiny, without which determination she would soon cease to believe in her own role and to be able to be useful to others, is incompatible with a defence organization in which she holds a subordinate position.

Consequently, without reneging on her membership in the Atlantic Alliance, between now and the ultimate date laid down for her obligations, which is 4 April 1969, France will continue progressively to modify the arrangements at present in force so far as they concern her. What she did yesterday in this respect in a number of fields she will do tomorrow in others, while, of course, taking the necessary steps to ensure that these changes are brought about progressively and without causing sudden inconvenience to her allies. Furthermore, she will hold herself ready to work out with them individually, following the method she has already employed in certain cases, the practical co-operative relationships which appear useful to them and to her, both in the immediate future and in the event of conflict. Naturally this goes for allied co-operation in Germany. In the aggregate it is a question of re-establishing a normal situation of sovereignty in which all French forces, whether on land, in the sky, or in the sea, as well as any foreign elements located in France, are in future responsible only to the French Authorities. That is to say, that what is involved, far from being a rupture, is merely a necessary adaptation.

Appendix V (abridged)

'Declaration on Strengthening Peace and Security in Europe'[1]

Bucharest Meeting of the Warsaw Pact, 5–8 July 1966

ONE

The safeguarding of a lasting peace and of security in Europe is in accord with the ardent desires of all peoples of the continent of Europe and is in the interests of universal peace. . . .

Now, two decades after the end of World War II, its consequences in Europe have not yet been liquidated, there is no German peace treaty and hotbeds of tension and abnormal situations in relations between states continue to exist.

The socialist states which signed the present Declaration believe that the elimination of this situation and the creation of firm foundations of peace and security in Europe assume that international relations proceeding from the renunciation of the threat of force or the use of force, and the need to settle international disputes only by peaceful means, should be based on the principles of sovereignty and national independence, equality and non-interference in domestic affairs and on respect of territorial inviolability.

The states of Europe should strive for the adoption of effective measures to prevent the danger of the start of an armed conflict in Europe and for the strengthening of European collective security. . . .

TWO

The growth of the forces which are coming out for the preservation and strengthening of peace is one of the determining features of the present international situation. . . .

Tendencies towards getting rid of the features of the cold war and the obstacles standing in the way of a normal development of European co-operation, for the settlement of outstanding issues through mutual understanding, for the normalization of international life and the *rapprochement* of peoples are increasingly appearing and developing in Europe. This course is opposed by imperialist re-

---

[1] Reprinted from *Survival*, September 1966, pp. 289–92.

actionary circles which, pursuing aggressive aims, strive to fan tensions and to poison relations between the European states.

A direct threat to peace in Europe and to the security of the European peoples is presented by the present policy of the United States of America. . . . The United States interferes in the domestic affairs of other states, violates the sacred right of every people to settle its own destiny, resorts to colonial repressions and armed intervention, hatches plots in various countries of Asia, Africa and Latin America, and everywhere supports reactionary forces and venal regimes that are hated by the peoples. There can be no doubt that the aims of the United States policy in Europe have nothing in common with the vital interests of the European peoples and the aim of European security.

The American ruling circles would like to impose their will on their allies in Western Europe and to make Western Europe an instrument of the United States global policy, which is based on the attempt to stop and even turn back the historic process of the national and social liberation of the peoples. Hence the attempts to involve some West European states in military ventures even in other parts of the world, and Asia in particular.

The United States aggressive circles, which have the support of the reactionary forces of Western Europe, are, with the help of the North Atlantic military *bloc* and the military machine created by it, trying further to deepen the division of Europe, to keep up the arms race, to increase international tensions and to impede the establishment and development of normal ties between the West European and East European states. . . .

The US policy in Europe, promoted during the post-war years, is the more dangerous for the European peoples in that it is increasingly based on collusion with the militaristic and revanchist forces of West Germany. These forces are openly pushing the United States to promote an even more dangerous course in Europe. This policy is reflected in the projected creation of a sort of alliance between the American imperialists and the West German revanchists.

The militaristic and revanchist circles of West Germany do not want to take the vital interests of the German people itself into account; they are pursuing aggressive aims which manifest themselves in all their actions—in the switching of the country's economic potential to military lines, in the creation of a Bundeswehr of 500,000 men in the glorification of the history of German conquests and in the nurturing of hatred towards other peoples whose lands are again being coveted by these circles in the Federal Republic of Germany.

At present the demand for the possession of nuclear weapons is the focal point of this policy. The creation in the Federal Republic of Germany of a scientific technical and industrial basis that would serve at a certain moment for the manufacture of their own atomic and nuclear bombs is being openly and secretly accelerated. By their joint efforts, the peace-loving countries and peoples have so far succeeded in delaying the creation of a NATO joint nuclear force which would give the Federal Republic of Germany access to nuclear weapons; but the plans for this have not been shelved.

The fundamental interests of all the peoples demand the renunciation of the plans for creating a NATO multilateral nuclear force. If, however, the NATO countries, acting contrary to the interests of peace, embark on a course of implementing the plans for creating a multilateral nuclear force or giving West Germany access to nuclear weapons in any form whatsoever, the member states of the Warsaw Treaty Organization would be compelled to carry out the defensive measures necessary to ensure their security.

The territorial claims of the West German revanchists must be emphatically rejected. They are absolutely without basis or prospects. The question of European frontiers has been solved finally and irrevocably. The inviolability of the existing frontiers between European states, including the frontiers of the sovereign German Democratic Republic, Poland and Czechoslovakia, is one of the main prerequisites for ensuring European security.

The states represented at the present meeting confirm their resolution to crush any aggression against them on the part of the forces of imperialism and reaction. For their part, the member states of the Warsaw Treaty Organization declare that they have no territorial claims whatever against a single state in Europe. The policy of revanchism and militarism, carried through by German imperialism, has always ended in fiasco. Given the present balance of forces in the world arena and in Europe, it is attended by irreparable consequences for the Federal Republic of Germany.

The interests of peace and security in Europe and throughout the world, like the interests of the German people, demand that the ruling circles of the Federal Republic of Germany take the real state of affairs in Europe into account, and this means that they take as their point of departure the existence of two German states, abandon their claims for the frontiers of Europe to be carved up again, abandon their claims to the right exclusively to represent the whole of Germany and their attempts to bring pressure to bear on states that recognize the German Democratic Republic, renounce the criminal Munich *diktat*, and acknowledge that it has been null and void from the very beginning. They must prove by deeds that they have really learned the lessons of history and that they will put an end to militarism and revanchism and will carry through a policy of the normalization of relations between states and the development of co-operation and friendship between peoples.

The German Democratic Republic, which is a major factor making for the safeguarding of peace in Europe, has addressed the government and Bundestag of the Federal Republic of Germany with constructive proposals: to renounce nuclear arms on a reciprocal basis, to reduce the armies of both German states, to assume a commitment not to use force against each other and to sit down at a conference table for a solution of the national problems of interest to both the German Democratic Republic and the Federal Republic of Germany which have developed. The government of the Federal Republic of Germany, however, evinces no interest in these proposals. The states which have signed this Declaration support this initiative of the German Democratic Republic.

Having examined all aspects of the present situation in Europe, the states represented at the meeting have drawn the conclusion that in Europe, where almost half the states are socialist, it is possible to prevent undesirable developments. The problem of European security can be solved by the joint efforts of the European states and all the public forces that are coming out for peace, irrespective of their ideological views and religious or other convictions. This task will be all the more successfully accomplished, the sooner the influence of those forces who would like to continue aggravating tension in the relations between European states is paralyzed. . . .

A major factor which increasingly complicates the carrying out of war gambles in Europe is the growth of the influence of these forces in the West European states which are aware of the need to rise above differences in political views and convictions and come out for a relaxation of international tension, for the comprehensive development of mutually advantageous relations between all the states of Europe without discrimination and for the complete independence of their countries and the maintenance of their national identity.

The states which have signed this Declaration note as a positive feature the presence of circles in the Federal Republic of Germany that come out against revanchism and militarism, which call for the establishment of normal relations with the countries of both the West and the East, including normal relations between both German states, and are pressing for a relaxation of international tension and the safeguarding of European security so that all Germans may enjoy the blessings of peace. . . .

THREE

The states that are signatories to this Declaration hold that measures for the strengthening of security in Europe can and should be taken, in the first instance, in the following main directions:

1. They call upon all European states to develop good-neighbourly relations on the basis of the principles of independence and national sovereignty, equality, non-interference in internal affairs and mutual advantage founded on the principles of peaceful co-existence between states with different social systems. Proceeding from this, they come out for the strengthening of economic and trade relations, the multiplication of contacts and forms of co-operation in science, technology, culture and art, as well as in other areas which provide new opportunities for co-operation among European countries. . . .

The development of general European co-operation makes it necessary for all states to renounce any kind of discrimination and pressure, either political or economic in nature, designed against other countries, and requires their equal co-operation and the establishment of normal relations between them, including the establishment of normal relations with both German states. The establishment and development of good-neighbourly relations between European states with different social systems can make their economic and cultural contacts more active and thus increase the possibilities for European states to make an effective contribution to improving the climate in Europe and the development of mutual confidence and respect.

2. The socialist countries have always and consistently come out against the division of the world into military *blocs* or alliances, and for the elimination of the dangers which flow from this for universal peace and security. The Warsaw Treaty of Friendship, Co-operation and Mutual Assistance—a defensive pact of sovereign and equal states—was concluded in reply to the formation of the military aggressive NATO alignment and the inclusion of West Germany into it. However, the member states of the Warsaw Treaty Organization have considered and consider now that the existence of military *blocs* and war bases on the territories of other states, which are imposed by the imperialist forces, constitute an obstacle along the road of co-operation between states.

A genuine guarantee of the security and progress of every European country must be the establishment of an effective security system in Europe, based on relations of equality and mutual respect between all states of the continent and on the joint efforts of all European nations—and not the existence of military alignments which do not conform with healthy tendencies in international affairs today. The countries that have signed this Declaration consider that the need has matured for steps to be taken towards the relaxation, above all, of military tension in Europe.

The governments of our states have more than once pointed out that in case of the discontinuance of the operation of the North Atlantic Alliance, the Warsaw Treaty would become invalid, and that their place ought to be taken by a European security system. They now solemnly reaffirm their readiness for the simultaneous abolition of these alliances.

If, however, the member states of the North Atlantic Treaty are still not ready to accept the complete dissolution of both alignments, the states that have signed this Declaration consider that it is already now expedient to reach an understanding on the abolition of the military organization, both of the North Atlantic Pact and of the Warsaw Treaty. At the same time, they declare that as long as the North Atlantic *bloc* exists, and aggressive imperialist circles encroach on world peace, the socialist countries represented at this meeting, maintaining high vigilance, are fully resolved to strengthen their might and defence potential. At the same time, we believe it necessary that all member states of the North Atlantic Pact and the Warsaw Treaty, and also the countries who do not participate in any military alliances, should exert efforts on a bilateral or multilateral basis with the object of advancing the cause of European security.

3. Great importance is now also assumed by such partial measures towards military relaxation on the European continent as the abolition of foreign war bases; the withdrawal of all forces from foreign territories to within their national frontiers; the reduction, on an agreed scale and at agreed deadlines, of the numerical strength of the armed forces of both German states; measures aimed at eliminating the danger of a nuclear conflict (the setting up of nuclear-free zones and the assumption of the commitment by the nuclear powers not to use these weapons against the states which are parties to such zones, etc.); and the ending of flights by foreign planes carrying atom or hydrogen bombs over the territories of European states and of the entry of foreign submarines and surface ships with nuclear arms on board into the ports of such states.

4. The states must concentrate their efforts on excluding the possibility of access of the Federal Republic of Germany to nuclear weapons in any form—directly, or indirectly through alignments of states—and to exclusive control or any form of participation in the control of such weapons. The way this problem is resolved will largely determine the future of the peoples of Europe, and not only the peoples of Europe. On this question, too, half-hearted decisions are impermissible.

5. The immutability of frontiers is the foundation of a lasting peace in Europe. The interests of the normalization of the situation in Europe demand that all states, both in Europe and outside the European continent, proceed in their foreign political actions from recognition of the frontiers that really exist between European states, including the Polish frontier on the Oder-Neisse line and the frontiers between the two German states.

6. A German peace settlement is in accord with the interests of peace in Europe. The socialist states which are represented at the meeting are ready to continue the search for the solution of this problem. This solution must take into consideration the interests of the security of all the countries concerned and the security of Europe as a whole.

A constructive approach to this question is only possible if it proceeds from reality, above all, from recognition of the fact of the existence of two German states—the German Democratic Republic and the Federal Republic of Germany. At the same time, such a settlement requires recognition of the existing frontiers and the refusal of both German states to possess nuclear weapons. . . .

As for the reunion of both German states, the way to this lies through the relaxation of tension, through a gradual *rapprochement* between the two sovereign German states and agreements between them, through agreements on disarmament in Germany and Europe and on the basis of the principle that when Germany is reunited, the united German state would be truly peaceful and democratic and would never again be a danger to its neighbours or to peace in Europe.

7. Convocation of a general European conference to discuss the questions of ensuring security in Europe and organizing general European co-operation would be of great positive importance. The agreement reached at the conference could be expressed, for example, in the form of a general European declaration on co-operation for the maintenance and strengthening of European security. Such a declaration could provide for an undertaking by the signatories to be guided in their relations by the interests of peace, to settle disputes by peaceful means only, to hold consultations and exchange information on questions of mutual interest and to contribute to the all-round development of economic, scientific, technical and cultural relations. The declaration should be open to all interested states to join.

The convocation of a conference on questions of European security and co-operation could contribute to the establishment of a system of collective security in Europe and would be an important land-mark in the contemporary history of Europe. Our countries are ready to take part in such a conference at any time convenient to the other interested states, both members of the North Atlantic Treaty and neutrals. Neutral European countries could also play a positive role in the convocation of such a meeting. It goes without saying that the agenda and other questions concerning the preparation of such a meeting or conference should be decided upon by all participating states together, bearing in mind the proposals submitted by every one of them.

The countries represented at this meeting are also prepared to use other methods available for discussing problems of European security: talks through diplomatic channels, meetings of Foreign Ministers or special representatives on a bilateral or multilateral basis and contacts at the highest level. They consider that the considerations above cover the principal, the most important, aspects of ensuring European security. They are also ready to discuss other proposals which have been submitted, or may be submitted by any state, for the solution of this problem. . . . The parties to this meeting are convinced that countries on the other continents, too, cannot be indifferent to how things develop in Europe.

The Organization of NATO

Extracted from the *NATO Handbook, April 1969*

THE COUNCIL AND THE DEFENCE PLANNING COMMITTEE (DPC)

The North Atlantic Council is the highest authority of the Alliance. It is composed of representatives of the fifteen member countries. These being sovereign states, equal in status, all decisions of the Council are taken unanimously. The Council may meet at the level either of Ministers or Permanent Representatives (holding the rank of Ambassador). At Ministerial Meetings of the Council, the members of the Alliance are represented by one—or several—of their ministers (for Foreign Affairs, Defence, Finance, Economic Affairs) according to the agenda of the meeting. In December 1957, the Council even met at the level of Heads of Government. The Council meets at Ministerial level at least twice a year: in the spring in the capital of one of the member countries, in the winter at NATO Headquarters in Brussels. Between Ministerial Sessions, the Permanent Representatives meet at least once a week—often more frequently—thus ensuring continuous consultation. The Council can be called together any time at short notice.

Whatever the level at which the Council meets, its chairman is the Secretary General of NATO. Each year the Foreign Minister of a member state is honorary President of the Council. This Presidency rotates annually according to alphabetical order in English.

Since the Organization of the North Atlantic Treaty is not supra-national, all decisions taken are the expressions of the *collective will of the member governments*. It is in the Council that the views of governments are exchanged on all major issues. Consultation covers political, military, economic and a wide range of other subjects. (To produce the same results through normal diplomatic channels, involving each country consulting the other 14, would require no less than 105 bilateral exchanges.)

Military policy matters are discussed at the same level in the

'Defence Planning Committee'. As in the Council, member countries are represented on this Committee by their Permanent Representatives. They meet round the same table as the Council and also under the same chairmanship of the Secretary General. Since the withdrawal of France from the integrated military organization in 1966, her representative does not attend these meetings.

THE PERMANENT REPRESENTATIVES AND DELEGATIONS

The Permanent Representatives are assisted by national Delegations also located at NATO Headquarters. The Delegations vary in size but the majority of them include officers specifically charged with representing their countries on the various specialized committees. Before a meeting of the Council notice is given of the agenda and any subjects to be discussed, so that representatives have time to seek the instructions of their governments.

THE COUNCIL COMMITTEES

In carrying out its role, the Council is assisted by Committees, some of a permanent nature, some temporary. Like the Council, the membership of each committee is made up of national representatives drawn from the delegations. They study questions submitted to them by the Council for assessment or recommendation. As in the case of decisions of the Council, committee decisions represent a *collective view of the fifteen governments based on the instructions those governments have sent to their representatives on the committees.* The most important committees are those dealing with the following matters: Political Affairs, Defence Review, Economic Affairs, Science, Infrastructure, Civil Emergency Planning, Information and Cultural Affairs, Military and Civil Budget Committees. Many other committees deal with specialized subjects, such as NATO pipelines, communications, European air space, etc.

Since 1966 the problems of nuclear defence are dealt with by the Nuclear Defence Affairs Committee (which is composed of all member countries, except France, Iceland, and Luxembourg, and which meets at the level of Permanent Representatives) and the Nuclear Planning Group (a Committee of seven members). Membership of the NPG changes so that member countries not possessing nuclear weapons have an opportunity, together with the nuclear powers, to participate in the planning of the nuclear defence measures of the Alliance as a whole.[1]

THE SECRETARY GENERAL AND THE INTERNATIONAL SECRETARIAT

The Secretary General is both Chairman of the North Atlantic Council and of the Defence Planning Committee at all levels. He is the head of the International Secretariat, whose staff is drawn from all member countries.

The Secretary General has the right to propose items for NATO consultation and he is generally responsible for promoting and directing the process of consultation. He has the authority to offer his good offices informally at any time in cases of disputes between member countries, and with their consent, to initiate or facilitate procedures of enquiry, mediation, conciliation or arbitration (for example recently with Greece and Turkey over Cyprus).

The Deputy Secretary General assists the Secretary General in his function and deputises for him in his absence. Under the Secretary General are four Assistant Secretaries General, each in charge of a division, as follows: Political Affairs, Defence Planning & Policy, Defence Support, and Scientific Affairs. Each Assistant Secretary General is normally chairman of the main committee dealing with his subject.

The Executive Secretary is Secretary to the North Atlantic Council and the Defence Planning Committee and is also responsible for Council Operations, Communications and Security.

There is a separate Office of Administration under a Director. The Financial Controller, who is appointed by the Council, is responsible for the control of expenditure.

THE MILITARY COMMITTEE AND COMMANDS

The Military Committee is the highest military authority in the Alliance and is responsible for making recommendations to the Council and Defence Planning Committee on military matters and for supplying guidance on military questions to Allied Commanders and subordinate military authorities. It is composed of the Chiefs-of-Staff of all member countries, except France. Iceland, having no

[1] On 1 March, 1969, the members of the Nuclear Planning Group were: Belgium, Denmark, Federal Republic of Germany, Greece, Italy, United Kingdom, United States.

military forces, may be represented by a civilian. The Chiefs-of-Staff meet at least twice a year—and whenever else it may be found necessary. However, to enable the Military Committee to function in permanent session with effective powers of decision, each Chief-of-Staff appoints a Permanent Military Representative. Between meetings of the Chiefs-of-Staff, their Permanent Military Representatives deal with and settle questions which come within the province of the Military Committee, except those which, by their nature and scope, require the approval of the Chiefs-of-Staff.

The Presidency of the Military Committee rotates annually in the alphabetical order of countries. The Chairmanship is held by a Permanent chairman, elected by the Committee for a period of two to three years.

The Military Committee is represented on the North Atlantic Council and has a number of NATO military agencies under its authority.

THE INTERNATIONAL MILITARY STAFF

The Military Committee is assisted by an integrated International Military Staff which is headed by a Director, selected from any of the member nations. The Director is assisted by a Vice Director with a special responsibility for nuclear matters, five Assistant Directors of flag or general officer rank, and the Secretary of the International Military Staff. The five Assistant Directors head the Divisions for Intelligence; Plans and Policy; Operations, Training and Organization; Logistics; and Communications and Electronics. As the executive agency of the Military Committee, the International Military Staff is charged with ensuring that the policies and decisions of the Military Committee are implemented as directed. In addition, the International Military Staff prepares plans, initiates studies and recommends policy on matters of a military nature.

THE NATO COMMANDS

The strategic area covered by the North Atlantic Treaty is divided, taking account of geographical and political factors, among three Commands: the Atlantic Ocean Command, the European Command and the Channel Command. (Defence plans for the North American area are developed by the Canada-US Regional Planning Group). The authority exercised by these Commands varies in form, being affected by the geographical and political factors and by the situation under peace or war conditions.

The forces of member countries remain under national command in peacetime; some of them may either be assigned or earmarked to NATO Commands.

The NATO Commanders are responsible for the development of defence plans for their respective areas, for the determination of force requirements and for the deployment and exercise of the forces under their Command.

The organization of these Commands is flexible enough and the liaison between them close enough to allow for mutual support in the event of war, and the rapid shifting of the necessary land, sea and air forces to meet any situation likely to confront the North Atlantic Community.

THE EUROPEAN COMMAND

Allied Command Europe (ACE) covers the area extending from the North Cape to the Mediterranean and from the Atlantic to the eastern border of Turkey, excluding the United Kingdom and Portugal, the defence of which does not fall under any one major NATO Command. ACE is subdivided into a number of subordinate Commands.[1]

The European area is under the Supreme Allied Commander Europe (SACEUR), whose headquarters, near Mons in Belgium, are known as SHAPE (Supreme Headquarters Allied Powers Europe).

The Supreme Commander has also under his orders the ACE Mobile Force. This force is composed of both land and air force units supplied by different member countries. It can be ready for action at very short notice in any threatened area and in particular on the northern and southern flanks of the European Command.

In peacetime SACEUR's main functions are to prepare and finalize defence plans for the area under his command, and ensure the combat efficiency of forces assigned to him in the event of war. SACEUR also makes recommendations to the Military Committee on matters likely to improve the organization of his command.

[1] ACE subordinate Commands are: the *Northern Europe Command* (Kolsas, Norway); the *Central Europe Command* (Brunssum, the Netherlands); the *Southern Europe Command* (Naples, Italy); the *UK Air Defence Region Command* (Stanmore, UK); and the *ACE Mobile Force* (Seckenheim, Fed. Rep. of Germany).

182

He would, in time of war, control all land, sea and air operations in this area. Internal defence (including that of Corsica, Sardinia and Sicily) and defence of coastal waters remain the responsibility of the national authorities concerned, but the Supreme Commander would have full authority to carry out such operations as he considered necessary for the defence of any part of the area under his Command.

Thirteen of the North Atlantic countries maintain a National Military Representative (NMR) at SHAPE, providing military liaison with the Allied Chief-of-Staff.

SACEUR and his Deputy Supreme Allied Commander are assisted by political and scientific advisers in addition to the usual military staff advisers.

THE ATLANTIC OCEAN COMMAND

This Command extends from the North Pole to the Tropic of Cancer and from the coastal waters of North America to those of Europe and Africa, except for the Channel and the British Isles. The Atlantic Ocean Command is subdivided into a number of subordinate commands.[1]

The Supreme Commander Atlantic also has under his orders the NATO Standing Naval Force Atlantic (STANAVFORLANT). This force is composed of an international squadron of ships from NATO countries normally operating in the Atlantic.

The Supreme Allied Commander Atlantic (SACLANT), like the Supreme Allied Commander Europe, receives his directions from the Military Committee.

SACLANT's peacetime responsibilities consist of preparing and finalizing defence plans, conducting joint training exercises, laying down training standards and supplying the NATO authorities with information on his strategic requirements.

The primary task in wartime of the Allied Command Atlantic is to ensure security in the whole Atlantic area by guarding the sea lanes and denying their use to an enemy. SACLANT has responsibility for islands in this area, such as Iceland and the Azores.

[1] Commands subordinate to the Supreme Allied Commander Atlantic are: the *Western Atlantic Command* (Norfolk, US); the *Eastern Atlantic Command* (Northwood, UK); the *Striking Fleet Atlantic* (Afloat); the *Submarines Allied Command Atlantic* (Norfolk, US); the *Iberian Atlantic Command* (Lisbon, Portugal); and the *Standing Naval Force Atlantic* (Afloat).

SACLANT's responsibilities are almost entirely operational. Unlike SACEUR, he has no forces permanently attached to his Command in peacetime. However, for training purposes and in the event of war, forces earmarked by the nations involved are assigned to his direction. Although these forces are predominantly naval, they also include ground forces and land-based air forces.

THE CHANNEL COMMAND AND THE CHANNEL COMMITTEE

The Channel Command covers the English Channel and the southern areas of the North Sea. Its mission is to control and protect merchant shipping in the area, co-operating with SACEUR in the air defence of the Channel. In emergency the forces earmarked to the Command are predominantly naval but include maritime air forces. The Allied Commander-in-Chief has a Maritime Air Adviser who is also the Commander Allied Maritime Air Force Channel.

The Channel Committee consists of the Naval Chiefs-of-Staff of Belgium, the Netherlands and the United Kingdom, and acts as an advisory body to the Allied Commander-in-Chief.

CANADA-UNITED STATES REGIONAL PLANNING GROUP

This Planning Group, which covers the North American area, develops and recommends to the Military Committee plans for the defence of the Canada-United States region. It meets alternately in Washington and Ottawa.

Appendix VII

Future Tasks of the Alliance

Report of the North Atlantic Council, *December 1967* (The Harmel Report)

1. A year ago, on the initiative of the Foreign Minister of Belgium, the governments of the fifteen nations of the Alliance resolved to 'study the future tasks which face the Alliance, and its procedures for fulfilling them in order to strengthen the Alliance as a factor for durable peace'. The present report sets forth the general tenor and main principles emerging from this examination of the future tasks of the Alliance.

2. Studies were undertaken by Messrs Schütz, Watson, Spaak, Kohler and Patijn. The Council wishes to express its appreciation and thanks to these eminent personalities for their efforts and for the analyses they produced.

3. The exercise has shown that the Alliance is a dynamic and vigorous organization which is constantly adapting itself to changing conditions. It also has shown that its future tasks can be handled within the terms of the Treaty by building on the methods and procedures which have proved their value over many years.

4. Since the North Atlantic Treaty was signed in 1949 the international situation has changed significantly and the political tasks of the Alliance have assumed a new dimension. Amongst other developments, the Alliance has played a major part in stopping Communist expansion in Europe; the USSR has become one of the two world super-powers but the Communist world is no longer monolithic; the Soviet doctrine of 'peaceful co-existence' has changed the nature of the confrontation with the West but not the basic problems. Although the disparity between the power of the United States and that of the European states remains, Europe has recovered and is on its way towards unity. The process of decolonization has transformed European relations with the rest of the world; at the same time, major problems have arisen in the relations between developed and developing countries.

5. The Atlantic Alliance has two main functions. Its first function is to maintain adequate military strength and political solidarity to deter aggression and other forms of pressure and to defend the territory of member countries if aggression should occur. Since its inception, the Alliance has successfully fulfilled this task. But the possibility of a crisis cannot be excluded as long as the central political issues in Europe, first and foremost the German question, remain unsolved. Moreover, the situation of instability and uncertainty still precludes a balanced reduction of military forces. Under these conditions, the Allies will maintain as necessary, a suitable military capability to assure the balance of forces, thereby creating a climate of stability, security and confidence.

In this climate the Alliance can carry out its second function, to pursue the search for progress towards a more stable relationship in which the underlying political issues can be solved. Military security and a policy of *détente* are not contradictory but complementary. Collective defence is a stabilizing factor in world politics. It is the necessary condition for effective policies directed towards a greater relaxation of tensions. The way to peace and stability in Europe rests in particular on the use of the Alliance constructively in the interest of *détente*. The participation of the USSR and the USA will be necessary to achieve a settlement of the political problems in Europe.

6. From the beginning the Atlantic Alliance has been a co-operative grouping of states sharing the same ideals and with a high degree of common interest. Their cohesion and solidarity provide an element of stability within the Atlantic area.

7. As sovereign states the Allies are not obliged to subordinate their policies to collective decision. The Alliance affords an effective forum and clearing house for the exchange of information and views; thus, each of the Allies can decide his policy in the light of close knowledge of each others' problems and objectives. To this end the practice of frank and timely consultations needs to be deepened and improved. Each Ally should play its full part in promoting an improvement in relations with the Soviet Union and the countries of Eastern Europe, bearing in mind that the pursuit of *détente* must not be allowed to split the Alliance. The chances of success will clearly be greatest if the Allies remain on parallel courses, especially in matters of close concern to them all; their actions will thus be all the more effective.

8. No peaceful order in Europe is possible without a major effort by all concerned. The evolution of Soviet and East European policies gives ground for hope that those governments may eventually come to recognize the advantages to them of collaborating in working towards a peaceful settlement. But no final and stable settlement in Europe is possible without a solution of the German question which lies at the heart of present tensions in Europe. Any such settlement must end the unnatural barriers between Eastern and Western Europe, which are most clearly and cruelly manifested in the division of Germany.

9. Accordingly the Allies are resolved to direct their energies to this purpose by realistic measures designed to further a *détente* in East-West relations. The relaxation of tensions is not the final goal but is part of a long-term process to promote better relations and to foster a European settlement. The ultimate political purpose of the Alliance is to achieve a just and lasting peaceful order in Europe accompanied by appropriate security guarantees.

10. Currently, the development of contacts between the countries of Western and Eastern Europe is now mainly on a bilateral basis. Certain subjects, of course, require by their very nature a multilateral solution.

11. The problem of German reunification and its relationship to a European settlement has normally been dealt with in exchanges between the Soviet Union and the three Western powers having special responsibilities in this field. In the preparation of such exchanges the Federal Republic of Germany has regularly joined the three Western powers in order to reach a common position. The other Allies will continue to have their views considered in timely discussions among the Allies about Western policy on this subject, without in any way impairing the special responsibilities in question.

12. The Allies will examine and review suitable policies designed to achieve a just and stable order in Europe, to overcome the division of Germany and to foster European security. This will be part of a process of active and constant preparation for the time when fruitful discussions of these complex questions may be possible bilaterally or multilaterally between Eastern and Western nations.

13. The Allies are studying disarmament and practical arms control measures, including the possibility of balanced force reduc-

tions. These studies will be intensified. Their active pursuit reflects the will of the Allies to work for an effective *détente* with the East.

14. The Allies will examine with particular attention the defence problems of the exposed areas e.g. the South-eastern flank. In this respect the current situation in the Mediterranean presents special problems, bearing in mind that the current crisis in the Middle East falls within the responsibilities of the United Nations.

15. The North Atlantic Treaty area cannot be treated in isolation from the rest of the world. Crises and conflicts arising outside the area may impair its security either directly or by affecting the global balance. Allied countries contribute individually within the United Nations and other international organizations to the maintenance of international peace and security and to the solution of important international problems. In accordance with established usage the Allies or such of them as wish to do so will also continue to consult on such problems without commitment and as the case may demand.

16. In the light of these findings, the Ministers directed the Council in permanent session to carry out, in the years ahead, the detailed follow-up resulting from this study. This will be done either by intensifying work already in hand or by activating highly specialized studies by more systematic use of experts and officials sent from capitals.

17. Ministers found that the study by the Special Group confirmed the importance of the role which the Alliance is called upon to play during the coming years in the promotion of *détente* and the strengthening of peace. Since significant problems have not yet been examined in all their aspects, and other problems of no less significance which have arisen from the latest political and strategic developments have still to be examined, the Ministers have directed the Permanent Representatives to put in hand the study of these problems without delay, following such procedures as shall be deemed most appropriate by the Council in permanent session, in order to enable further reports to be subsequently submitted to the Council in Ministerial Session.